A Dog Called DEZ

THE TRUE STORY OF HOW ONE AMAZING DOG CHANGED HIS OWNER'S LIFE

John Tovey
with Veronica Clark

Published by John Blake Publishing Ltd,
3 Bramber Court, 2 Bramber Road,
London W14 9PB, England

www.johnblakepublishing.co.uk

www.facebook.com/johnblakebooks 🆕
twitter.com/jblakebooks 🆕

First published in hardback in 2013
This paperback edition published in 2014

ISBN: 978-1-78418-007-2

British Library Cataloguing-in-Publication Data:

A catalogue record for this book is available from the British Library.

Design by www.envydesign.co.uk

Printed in Great Britain by CPI Group (UK) Ltd

5 7 9 10 8 6 4

Papers used by John Blake Publishing are natural, recyclable products made
from wood grown in sustainable forests. The manufacturing processes conform
to the environmental regulations of the country of origin.

Every attempt has been made to contact the relevant copyright-holders,
but some were unobtainable. We would be grateful if the appropriate
people could contact us.

Called
DEZ

Donations to Guide Dogs can be
made online via John Tovey's JustGiving page:
www.justgiving.com/John-Tovey

For further information,
see 'Please Help' on page 278.

In memory of my wonderful friend David Evans,
and Anthony, my loving brother
RIP.

Contents

Introduction

I TRULY BELIEVED when I lost my sight, that my life was over. I was wrong. With my amazing guide dog Dez by my side it was just beginning. Dez's arrival would be the start of everything, a truly pivotal moment in my life, and one I would share with my best four-legged friend.

It'd been a long journey along a rocky path. Life before Dez had been pretty bleak and I'd not been a very good person at all. As you will come to read in this book, Dez turned out to be my redemption. There will be bits of my story when you will judge me, and rightly so, I wasn't a nice guy. There'll other parts when you won't like me very much but that's okay too because I didn't like myself very much either. My life wasn't a good one. I was a bad lad, as pure and simple as that. I lashed out and betrayed all those who ever loved or tried to help me; everyone apart from Dez. When I lost my sight I pushed them all away again, but life is strange and sometimes it takes the loss of everything to make you value what you've got and realise just how lucky you truly are.

I still don't think I deserve Dez (and I know the poor lad certainly doesn't deserve me) but I think we were meant to meet so we could discover together what life is about. By this, I don't mean possessions or material things, I mean love and friendship but most of all, I mean trust. I trust Dez with my life and every day, he holds it in his paw. We depend on one another. My beautiful Dez is like my right arm. He's my eyes and my guide. He is my life.

I don't seek sympathy because today I'm happy and content with life. My blindness has introduced me to some of the most incredible people I've ever met, including everyone at Guide Dogs, and I feel lucky to call them my friends. Although I'm totally blind, in many ways I can see clearly for the first time in my life. Life is for living and I don't want to waste another minute of it.

So, here is the story of how a schmuck like me got so lucky that he ended up with the best dog in the world. Here is my story, warts and all. I hope you like it. Here is *A Dog Called Dez*.

CHAPTER ONE

Four-Legged Friend

PACING UP AND down the room, I pressed the button on the speaking clock which was standing in the middle of the coffee table. Another few minutes and they'd be here. My hands patted over surfaces as I felt my way around the place doing a last minute check. The floor was clear. His toys were in the corner near his new bed. His food was bagged up and ready to go in the kitchen – a fortnight's supply in daily doses – enough to keep him going. Everything was set and ready for his arrival; now all I needed was the man himself, my new guide dog Dez. From this moment on he'd become my best friend, companion, confidant, eyes, ears and general life-saver. He'd be my Dez.

I flopped back down onto the sofa and sighed as I realised just how far I'd come to reach this point. For a moment I doubted my ability to look after a dog, I had trouble looking after myself so how on earth was I going to look after a five-stone Labrador? Just getting out of the house would be a challenge and then there'd be all that dog walking. I rubbed my head anxiously, was I up to the job? But as soon as I thought of him, a smile spread across my face. Of course I was, I couldn't wait!

In many ways I'd been waiting for this all my life – the moment I could take responsibility for someone else and now it had finally arrived.

I'd walked a long and rocky path to get to this point. To be honest I was amazed I was still living and breathing to tell the tale. Up until now I'd been hell-bent on destroying everything in my life and I'd almost succeeded. I'd been a selfish thug, not a nice person at all, but fate threw it all back in my face and now here I was, only something had changed because now I was blind. For the first time ever I felt vulnerable. After a lifetime of feeling angry at the world, I needed help.

The tables had turned and now I was at the mercy of others and I knew how it felt to be completely defenceless. Losing my sight and the ability to come and go as I pleased had floored me. My total loss of sight had quite literally knocked the stuffing out of me. I wondered if I deserved it, maybe this was punishment for all the bad things I'd done. If so, I hoped and prayed that my new guide dog Dez would lead me to a better and happier place.

I pressed the clock again; another ten minutes had ticked by and still no sign.

Where could they be?

My hands knotted nervously in my lap as I tried to keep calm and stop the butterflies from rising inside my stomach. I thought how strange it would feel having someone to look after and love again. An animal gives you a kind of unconditional and trusting love that only they and perhaps children can give. I'd already experienced this with my son James, a wonderful boy, despite his old man. Luckily, James had had a great mum in my ex-wife Tracey, and so had grown up to be a brilliant young man. How had I got so lucky? In many ways, sitting there waiting for Dez felt like becoming a father for the second time. Only this time I'd have to be his 'mum' too. I allowed myself a little chuckle. If only my old skinhead mates could see me now, they'd think I was soft in the head. I was, and it felt fantastic.

But this wasn't our first meeting. Dez and I had met briefly before. My guide dog trainer – a lovely woman called Emma Yard – had pulled a fast one. In order to get my own guide dog I'd been put on a waiting list. In the meantime, I trained hard for the day when I finally had a dog of my own.

One day, Emma took me out with another guide dog called Volley on a practice walk. Shortly after, we trained again. I presumed the dog she'd brought along was the same Volley but I was wrong and she didn't put me right. Instead she observed and, although I couldn't see her, I guessed that she'd nodded her head in approval. I should've realised from the start that this dog was different. For starters, unlike Volley he seemed a little more eager on the harness. He also had more character and walked faster along the street. By the end, I felt a little out of breath but totally elated at how well the training session had gone. In celebration, I stooped down to stroke who I thought was Volley but his fur felt different, kind of softer somehow. I smelt a rat.

'John,' Emma began. I thought I could hear mirth in her voice.

'Yes,' I replied, straightening up. Although I couldn't see her I automatically looked towards where her voice was coming from.

'You know I said I might have a dog for you?'

'Hmm,' I answered – something fishy was definitely going on here.

'Well, this is him. This is a dog called Dez, and I think he's the dog for you.'

I put my hand to my mouth and gasped. I'd been on the list waiting for my very own guide dog for over a year and he was finally here. He'd been walking with me for the past hour and I hadn't even realised.

'Hello mate,' I laughed as I bent down and reintroduced myself.

A grateful wet nose pushed against my hand.

'Well, you kept that quiet, didn't you?' I said, pretending to scold Emma who started to laugh.

'John, I just knew how nervous you'd get if I told you who you were really walking with. Dez is exactly the same and I couldn't have you both a bundle of nerves.'

I chuckled some more and got down on my knees and tickled Dez behind the back of his ears. My gorgeous new buddy leaned in against my hand gratefully, loving all the attention.

'What does he look like Emma?' I was desperate to know.

'Well, he's a gorgeous black Labrador, and right now he's looking at you with his big brown eyes.'

'Is he?' I said holding out my hand to touch his face. From nowhere a big, wet, slobbery tongue licked the back of it.

'I can't believe it,' I said shaking my head. 'Really, is he mine, all mine, to keep?'

4

'He is, John.'

'Yes!' I shouted punching the air.

I didn't care if I looked like an idiot, a blind man kneeling in the middle of the street next to a dog, almost crying with joy. Dez was here and now everything would be alright: life would be worth living again.

'Come on you two,' Emma said. Let's walk back home.'

On the way, Emma explained that she usually did a couple of 'match' walks but Dez and I had been so perfect together that she knew we'd be just fine. She was right. Ours was a match made in heaven. And now I knew he would be arriving for good any moment, my boy wonder, my Dez.

I anxiously pressed the button on the speaking clock. It was almost 7pm.

Where were they?

I started to fret; they were half an hour late.

What if something's wrong or they've been involved an accident?

I felt sick.

What if Emma's changed her mind?

I was just starting to worry when my thoughts were interrupted by a loud buzzing noise coming from the wall – it was the intercom. It was time.

I shot to my feet so quickly that I almost tripped myself up.

Calm down John, I told myself. *Remember to breathe.*

I repeated it over and over in my head but inside my heart was thumping with excitement. It felt like all my Christmases had come at once. This was it, Dez was here. I tapped my fingers along the wall until I located the intercom phone. I picked it up and heard a slight crackle and then the sound of a familiar voice.

'Hi John, its Emma. I've got someone here who's really looking forward to meeting you again!'

A ridiculous grin spread across my face. Just then I heard a whimper down the line.

It was him.

I felt a knot of anxiety in the pit of my stomach.

What if Dez decided he didn't like me?

Suddenly, I started to feel a little nervous.

'I'll just buzz you in,' I said, releasing the door. Despite my fears, I couldn't stop smiling. Moments later there was a tap at the door and I almost ran to open it.

'Hi John,' Emma said breezily. 'Here he is. Here's Dez.'

I listened out for all crucial signs.

If his paws drag on the floor it means he doesn't want to be here, a voice niggled inside my head.

I listened so hard that my ears hurt. But there was no dragging sound or even the slightest hesitation. Instead his claws clacked as they scrambled against laminate to get through the door as quickly as possible. I felt a whoosh of air against my leg and then he was gone.

'Someone's happy to be here,' Emma giggled as she followed him in through the door. As I closed it behind her my ears strained for his footsteps.

Where was he now?

Suddenly a noise came from the front room. I guessed he was over by his new bed; the squeak of a toy pierced the air.

'He's found his toys!' I grinned, listening out for more.

'He's got one in his mouth,' Emma said, filling in the gaps.

The door swung back on its hinges and bounced off the wall as nails skidded against the laminate in the hallway, outside the bedroom. Another door banged open.

Bedroom? I guessed.

Emma laughed and confirmed I was right.

'He's having a good sniff!'

'Hey, Dez, watch out for any dirty socks!' I called.

Then he was off again. I felt the whip of his tail against me in the hallway as he fled into the next bedroom and sussed that out too. Another whoosh of air rose up as he brushed past and I heard the tell-tale creak of the old bathroom door.

'That's the toilet mate, but it's mine, not yours,' I chuckled.

Emma laughed. Dez walked past me again but this time he stopped just inside the kitchen doorway. I heard the sound of him sniffing the air.

'Has he seen his food?' I asked. I'd left it piled up on the side of the kitchen worktop.

'No,' she replied, 'but I reckon he can smell it!'

I smirked. So it was true what they said about Labradors: lovely but greedy.

'No, it's not dinner time just yet,' I said, holding my hands low down to feel for him. His fur ran through my fingertips like silk, and he was off again. He whizzed by so quickly that I felt myself stumble slightly.

'Steady,' Emma said, holding my elbow.

'Blimey, he's like an earthquake!' I laughed.

It was true. Dez was a wonderful but earth-shattering new arrival – he was just what I needed. This four-legged little fella had exploded into my world and now he was about to turn it completely on its head.

'Dez,' I called. I heard his paws stop as he turned and gently padded back towards me. He'd seen enough, he'd done his tour of the flat. As I stroked him I felt his torso swing from side to side with the weight of his mighty wagging tail. I felt reassured. He was home and he felt and sounded happy to be here.

'Hello mate,' I said dipping down and stretching out a tentative hand. Dez's nose made contact first, a wet ball in the middle of my cupped warm palm. My fingers splayed out to touch his fur; it was just as I remembered, soft, fresh, thick and glossy beneath my touch.

'This is your new home Dez. I hope you're going to like it here.' I whispered in his ear.

Soft fur pressed close against my face as if he was listening to every word. I was so grateful I could've cried. It was an emotional moment for us both. Up until now, I'd been a lost soul, a burden to my friends, family and to society as a whole. But now I had Dez, and now life was going to be very different. I'd been waiting for this moment for so long that now it had finally arrived, I could barely believe it. But I'd been well prepared. In the week leading up to it, I'd travelled with a neighbour to an out of town pet shop to stock up on supplies and a bed for Dez to sleep in. Nothing cheap, it had to be the biggest and very best they had. But when the man in the shop asked me how big it needed to be I found myself a little stumped. I'd met Dez but I couldn't tell the man what size he was because I'd never seen him, so I guessed from memory.

'He's about this big,' I said holding my hand off the floor. 'And he's a Lab, about 18-months-old.'

Then there was the array of soft toys to choose from.

'Something with a squeak,' I told the man. 'I want him to have fun.'

Soon we had a mountain of them for him to play with. Then we picked out various bones to chew and his very own dog bowl.

And now he was here.

'I hope you're gonna like it here,' I said later as he settled down.

I rested a hand against the fur on his back and, although I already knew it from our first meeting, it was love at first touch. I was simply love struck.

Emma stayed for an hour to observe and generally lay down a few ground rules.

'Remember John, don't let him jump up on the bed or the furniture. Let him out in the back garden for a wee but no taking him out, not just yet. See how you two get on together.'

Suddenly, I heard her get up.

'Right,' she said. 'I'll see you two on Monday. Just have a chilled weekend together getting to know one another.'

'Oh, we will,' I replied patting Dez, who leaned in against me. 'We'll be fine, I just know we will.'

Emma made a fuss of Dez, and then she was gone. Now it was just the two of us. Dez and me. He brought me toys and, with no one there to watch him, tried to get me involved in an impromptu game of tug of war. He won. Finally, around 10pm, I heard his paws pad across the floor and the sound of him slumping down in his bed. He was exhausted. It had been quite a day for both of us. I remembered what Emma had said about not letting him on the furniture so I sat on the floor next to him and rested the palm of my hand against his back as he curled up.

'We'll do this together,' I whispered, stroking him lovingly behind the back of his ear. 'We're gonna be a team now Dezzy boy, and together we'll take on the world.'

Half an hour later, I was still stroking his fur when I heard a deep sigh. I leaned in closer and felt his breath against my face – Dez was snoring.

'Right, I'll take that as my cue,' I whispered getting quietly to my feet. 'Night, night boy.'

The excitement must have been too much for us both because within minutes I was asleep too. Normally, I'm a night owl, a bit of an insomniac, never able to sleep, but now I was just well, dog tired. Still, with Dez on my mind, I woke in the middle of the night to check on my little boy. I tiptoed towards his bed and placed a hand gently against his ribcage to check he was still breathing. He was. Reassured, I held my hand there and felt the soft *thud-thud* of his heart. It was ridiculous but now I was like an over-protective new mum, so I repeated it four or five times just to be sure. Exhaustion gripped me and eventually I fell into a deep sleep. The following morning, I was awoken by what I first thought was police breaking into my flat with a battering ram. Something solid hammered against wood until...

DOOF!

The door flung violently open and bounced off the wall. Then the scramble of dog claws against laminate flooring and then the weight of a greedy Labrador landing on top of me with a thump. Rule number one – 'no dogs on bed' – well and truly broken.

'Dez!' I gasped, screaming for mercy as my beautiful boy proceeded to dig against the duvet, shifting and pulling it back, exposing me, naked except for a pair of boxer shorts, for all the world to see.

'Wait, in a min...' I said trying to grab some clothes but it was too late. The duvet was hanging off the bed as the cold morning air hit my skin. I tried to move but was immediately bowled over by Dez pinning me down. His whole body was shaking with the weight of his wagging tail. Suddenly, and from nowhere, a wet nose pushed up underneath my chin.

'Okay, okay, I'm getting up!' I laughed, running my fingers through my hair.

I stretched my arms above my head and yawned.

What time was it? I couldn't tell for sure but it sounded quiet outside and far too early for my liking.

My hand fumbled along the bedside cabinet searching for the talking clock.

'*Seven-a-m.*' The words sounded too loud and brightly for my liking.

'What?' I muttered. 'Really?'

Dez scurried off but was back seconds later, this time his soggy nose pushed under my hand literally forcing me up.

'Okay boy, okay,' I laughed. This was mad!

I placed my feet flat on the floor at the side of the bed just to get him off my case.

'See, I'm moving, honest!'

Dez whimpered with delight and I could sense his excitement as his tail continued to whip against the wooden door.

'I'm up, look!' I protested as Dez continued to nudge, nuzzle and generally bully me out of bed and into action. There was a mad dash, paws against the floor and the sound of skidding as Dez came to a halt somewhere in the distance. I guessed he was sitting in the kitchen, waiting with anticipation beside his food bowl.

'Hungry are we?' I smiled as I padded my bare feet against the cold floor. 'Okay then, let's see what we've got for you.'

My hands felt along the surface until I located it. I undid the top of one of the plastic bags – a morning's food allowance

11

weighed exactly for his size and age. Yvonne Dutton, Dez's boarder at Guide Dogs had done it for me. I hadn't thought about it before now but, if I didn't want him to get fat, I'd have to save up enough money to buy myself a set of talking scales. I felt for his bowl with my other hand as the food spilled out from the bag. I worried I'd missed it. What if food was scattered all over the kitchen floor? But I needn't have worried. Within seconds Dez had hoovered up the entire lot.

'All gone?' I asked him, my fingertips feeling inside the empty food bowl. The bridge of his nose pushed against my hand, begging for a second portion.

'Oh no you don't!' I scolded gently. 'I might be blind but I ain't no mug. You've had your breakfast, you're not getting seconds.'

Once Dez realised I wasn't a pushover, he ran off to the front room in search of a toy. Meanwhile, I went to get washed and dressed. As the toy squeaked in his mouth, I tucked into some breakfast and poured myself a hot cup of coffee.

Moments later, his tail was wagging, knocking against the glass of the patio door: he wanted to go outside. I opened it and listened for him. I threw a toy and he brought it straight back so I threw another. This was fun! After a while I left the door open and flopped back down on the sofa. I pressed the other speaking clock, the one I kept in the middle of the coffee table, and waited for the time.

'*Eight-a-m,*' it announced.

Obscene! I was up, showered, dressed, and I'd even eaten my breakfast but it was still only 8am!

A dog called Dez had entered my life like a fabulous whirlwind. My lonely little flat had become a playground overnight, bursting and bouncing with happiness. How sad and empty my life had been before, I thought. But now Dez had come along and changed all that.

However, to get to this part you have to go right back to the start to where my story begins…

CHAPTER TWO

Home is Where the Hurt is

SITTING ON THE sofa, I kept quiet as quiet as a mouse as Dad watched the cricket on TV. He consumed a cigarette. As he did so, blue plumes of smoke rose up and billowed out, creating a thick blanket of smog which hung in mid-air. It choked at the back of my throat but I was too scared to cough. No one made a noise when Dad was watching TV, especially cricket.Just then, the back door slammed shut – it was Mum. She called out to me.

'John, come here. I've got something for you,' she shouted, her voice loud and clear down the hallway and into the room.

Dad swore and cursed her. I automatically flinched as he got up out of his chair and stormed over to the TV. He twisted the knob until the volume was deafening. Cricket was a quiet game but the TV was on so loud that you could hear the birds tweeting in the background. It was my signal to disappear. Whenever Dad got angry I knew it was best to get out. I sloped past him and made my way to the kitchen to see what Mum wanted. I walked into the kitchen but my heart sank when I spotted her hands – they were full of old carrier bags. It made me shudder because it meant one thing: she'd been shopping.

''Ere, I've got something for you,' she muttered searching through the top of each bag. Whatever it was, I didn't want it because I knew what was coming.

A few seconds later, she smiled to herself and pulled out a putrid green-coloured jumper which looked old, bobbled and worn out.

'Ah, this one's yours,' she exclaimed. 'Here, catch.'

She threw the bulging bag across towards me. As it sailed through the air, one of the jumper's sleeves flopped out as if trying to escape. With a heavy heart I surveyed the awful contents inside.

'Don't say thanks then, you ungrateful little bastard,' she snapped.

Tears pricked at the back of my eyes. She always called me that. I was always the 'little bastard' of the family. And I felt it.

'Come here you little bastard,' Mum called time and time again. I hated it. 'Little bastard' was my nickname and it stuck with me throughout my life.

'Well?' Mum asked, tapping her fingers on the kitchen table. 'What do you say to your Mum for buying you all those new things?'

'Thanks Mum,' I replied with a weak smile.

They're hardly new, I thought to myself.

Satisfied with her thank you, Mum sniffed and turned her attention towards the other bags resting on the kitchen table.

'Now, go and fetch your brother, I've got a bag for him too.'

I nodded, slunk out and wandered upstairs. I twisted the top of the plastic bag closed in my fingers. It wasn't to keep the clothes in, but to stop the jumble sale smell from leaking out. I eyed my brother Anthony as I walked into the bedroom. As soon as he spotted the bag in my hand his face fell.

'Oh no,' he groaned, 'has she been shopping again?'

'Afraid so,' I replied as Anthony squirmed.

I flopped down onto my bed and untwisted the bag. I tried not to breathe in too deeply but the stench of other people's body odour hit me as soon as I opened up the bag. I pinched the end of my nose and started to drag stuff out.

'Go on then, let's see what she's got you this time.' Anthony sighed. He looked as apprehensive as me.

'Urggh! Look at the colour of that jumper!' he yelled as soon as I pulled out the hideous woollen top.

'I know,' I huffed, rolling my eyes. 'Oh, by the way, Mum wants you to go downstairs because she's got a bag for you too.'

Anthony shuddered and went downstairs He knew he was in for the same thing – other people's cast-offs, all with the same tell-tale stale smell. Even though people had given them away, we'd be expected to wear them, unwashed, until they fell apart at the seams. We were well known in the area – the jumble sale kids – me, Anthony, and my two sisters. We were part of a unique gang and one that no one wanted to belong to.

As I unpacked the bag I felt something solid resting at the bottom. I searched around with my hand and felt some string. I twisted it around my fingers and pulled hard. Out popped a pair of worn, but cool white and blue trainers. Bingo! Maybe jumble sale clothes weren't so bad after all.

'Hmm, not bad,' I said, sizing them up in my hands.

At least they were better than the usual crap Mum bought me. I turned them over and checked the size, bollocks! They were one size too small, but they'd have to do. They felt tight and cramped against my feet but at least someone had already bedded them in. Just then, Anthony walked back in and caught me trying them on.

'Nice trainers,' he noted.

'Yeah, they're a bit tight,' I moaned, but realising he'd try and stake a claim on them I quickly changed my tone, 'they're okay though, at least they're comfy.'

Anthony shrugged as if he didn't care.

'Huh, I hope the person before didn't have verrucas,' he teased with a grin.

'Urggh, don't!' We began to laugh. We laughed long and hard at the ridiculous clothes. We laughed because no matter how bad things got, or how poor we were, we would always have each other. I loved my brother so much. Even though I was always the little bastard and he was Dad's favourite, it didn't matter because it wasn't his fault. Not only did he share Dad's name, he shared his heart along with my two sisters. Whatever happened, Anthony couldn't do any wrong in Dad's eyes. I was the disappointment. In fact, I was such a disappointment that I started to believe them when they told me. Maybe it was my destiny to grow up from being a little bastard to a big one?

'You'll never do anything good in your life, you little bastard.' Mum said. The same old mantra repeated day after day, and week after week, until I believed it. Maybe this was all I was good for. Maybe it was all I deserved.

Later that day, I folded my jumble sale clothes up neatly

and placed them inside my drawer. There was no point in asking Mum to wash them first.

'Wear them to school, they're good clothes them,' she insisted.

On the Monday, I got out of bed and dressed myself in my 'new' second-hand clothes, which stunk of other people's smells. I hoped that by the end of the day, through wear alone they'd pick up my body scent and become mine. I looked under the bed, pulled out the trainers and put them on. That's when I noticed that the left one was split at the seam, right across my little toe. I stood up in them to see if it was noticeable. It was. In fact, every time I took a step, the split opened and closed like a small mouth. I shifted my foot and tried to walk so it wasn't as obvious. But it was no use because, whatever I did, the gap seemed to get wider with every step I took. I had to think of something, fast. I decided to tell anyone who asked that I'd torn them playing football in the back garden. Thankfully, we didn't wear a uniform at my junior school otherwise who knows what Mum would've dressed us in. That morning I walked in proudly wearing my cool shoes and hoped that someone, anyone would notice.

'Cool trainers John,' a mate called over.

'Thanks,' I replied with a grin.

By the end of the first lesson most of my class had noticed I was wearing something nice for a change.

'I like your shoes,' a pretty girl said as she brushed passed me towards her desk.

'Cheers,' I replied, feeling ten feet tall. At last, I had something trendy, something everyone liked and wanted. But they weren't as comfy as I first thought. As the morning wore on my feet swelled and the leather bit in against them even tighter. It felt as though my toes were slowly being strangled but I hid my pain because for once, I was just like everyone else, and I didn't want to mess it up.

The bell rang for playtime. We all stood up, filed out of the classroom and ran over to the playground. Kids darted everywhere as we charged around and chased one another. Suddenly, an older lad marched up to me and poked me hard in the chest.

'Hey, they're my trainers,' he announced.

My heart sank. I had known this moment would come but I just didn't want it to be today.

'No, they're not. They're mine.' I insisted.

The boy looked puzzled and stooped down low to inspect my feet.

'Yep, they're definitely mine. Look, they're even split on that side like mine were.' He pointed towards the split trainer.

I twisted my feet in awkwardly suddenly feeling very self-conscious.

'No, they're definitely mine. I did that playing football,' I lied. I couldn't stand the humiliation.

'No, you didn't,' he shouted, raising his voice so that everyone could hear.

A gang of kids surrounded us.

'Those are my trainers. My mum gave them to the jumble sale, so your mum must have bought them for you. Look everyone, John Tovey wears jumble sale clothes! Ha ha! Tovey's the jumble sale kid!'

The other kids began to laugh and jeer and point at my shoes. I wanted the ground to swallow me whole.

'Urggh, John Tovey's smelly!' the pretty girl from my class sneered, pulling a face at the back.

'Yeah, Tovey only wears jumble sale clothes 'cos his mum and dad are so poor, they can't afford to buy him proper clothes,' the first lad continued.

'He stinks!' said another joining in.

A rage boiled up inside me and soon my fists were flying everywhere. I lashed out at them all, particularly the boy who had owned the shoes. Yet, try as I might, after that day the name 'smelly' stuck. I was smelly John Tovey who lived in a stinking house with rubbish in the garden and a dad who shouted so loud that he scared all the kids in the neighbourhood. My friends were so frightened that they never came round to call. Dad had been a parade sergeant in the army so he was used to shouting at people and he believed discipline was the key to bringing up his kids. However, all he did was scare the living daylights out of me. Looking back, it's obvious he shouldn't have left the army. He was like a fish out of water, living in a council house with a depressed wife and four children. I was the eldest boy so I tended to get it more in the neck than the others because I was 'old enough to know better'. Only I wasn't. Dad worked hard, he was a real grafter who could turn his hand to anything but it didn't make him happy. Most days he'd be out, working from early morning until late evening, just to bring in a wage, but the long hours made him constantly tired and grumpy. In return, he had a hair-trigger temper that would erupt at any moment. When it did, you knew better than to hang around.

Mum was altogether different. She was lazy and would mope around the house chain-smoking. Again, with hindsight, I realise she was depressed but no one spoke about things like that back then. This was the 1970s, and 'depression' didn't exist. Depression was something loonies had and they were locked up, away from 'normal' folk, where they couldn't hurt anyone. But Mum was depressed and somehow, she slowly lost the will to look after us.

As children we were always well fed but our food always came out of a tin. If it could be opened with a tin opener then it was dinner. We never ate any fresh food because it cost too much. The house was always cluttered and messy with bags of old clothes – it was an absolute pigsty. The TV was on all day but it never had any children's programmes on it because it was always tuned into whatever my parents wanted to watch, usually cricket for Dad, and Crossroads for Mum. They didn't even turn it off when we had visitors; it was just there in the background, like a wall of noise chatting away to itself through a constant fog of fag smoke. Not that we had many visitors. Our only regular visitor was a lady who ran the catalogue. She was clean, attractive and always had a full face of makeup on. She smelt nice too. Whenever she called around I'd snuggle up to her as if she was my own mum. Deep down, I wished she was because she looked just like a 'normal' mum should. I was so starved of love and attention that I'd press myself in tight and try to wrap my arms around her. She'd politely peel me off but I'd do it again and again. In the end, she let me just so she could get her order down and leave. In a sad way I think she got used to me, the strange little boy in the stinking house desperate to play happy families with her.

Mum came from Liverpool but her family were Irish born and bred. Her parents frowned upon her when she told them that she wanted to marry my father, an English soldier. But marry they did, just a few weeks later. My sister Clair was born on an army barracks near Dusseldorf, Germany, and I followed a year or so later, entering the world at the Wendover Maternity Hospital at Downend, just a stone's throw from where cricket legend WG Grace was born. I was proud to be born there, even if just by accident of birth. Anthony, the apple of Dad's eye, came next, followed by my youngest sister. Being the eldest boy, I was always sent on errands, usually to the local shop to buy cigarettes. I went from a very young age but I was never alone, our dog Skippy would always come with me. Skippy was a soft Collie-Labrador cross and I loved him to bits; we all did. But Skippy was also quite a character and very independent. He never walked on a lead – probably because we didn't own one – instead he'd simply walk by my side. I loved Skippy. In many ways, he was my confidant and my best friend when things got tough.

We lived on Park Avenue, in Frampton Cotterell, a small village on the outskirts of Bristol. It was a close-knit community where everyone knew their neighbours because we were all in the same boat. Poverty was rife but, unlike us, our neighbours were proud and kept their homes and gardens neat and tidy. Our garden was an embarrassment, overgrown with long grass, brambles and blackberry bushes. It was so bad it looked like a jungle, but it also served a useful purpose if you ever needed to hide. You could get lost in our garden because, as well as being totally overgrown, it was littered with sheets of corrugated iron, bags of old clothes, and stinking rubbish. It looked like the local tip.

Once, one of our cats gave birth to a litter. As they grew, one of the kittens decided he'd had enough of the constant shouting at home. He must have been a particularly sensitive soul because he decided to up sticks and go to live with the family across the road. They gladly took him and he remained there for the rest of his natural life. I always thought how smart he'd been but his cunning didn't stop there. Every time he saw a member of our family walk down the street he'd duck and hide; I think he was terrified we'd make him go back. If it was obvious to a kitten, it must have been obvious to everyone else. I always believed you could tell ours was a sad home just from walking past. It was unloved and neglected, just like the occupants inside.

One of my earliest memories was coveting a beautiful purple matchbox car that another boy owned. I was only four but as soon as he started showing it off to the rest of the class I decided to make it mine. When he refused to hand it over I snatched it. He cried, so I hit him on the nose. When Mum picked me up later that day the teacher was waiting for her and as soon as she heard what I'd done she smacked me. But it wasn't over because then she told Dad, and I got it twice as much. They called me a 'little bastard' and the name stuck. I was always in the wrong so I didn't try to be good anymore.

Even though I was small for my age, if someone had something I wanted I'd simply smack them to get it. I learnt fast. Soon I was pinching comics, sweets and anything else I could lay my thieving little hands on. My parents were dismayed and, in a bid to teach me a lesson, they decided to take a strong hand with me. If dinner was being served, I'd have to wait until last to get fed. It hurt me deeply and, instead of rehabilitating me, it caused me to go off the rails even more.

Mum tried her best to hold down various jobs. She cleaned in a pub and even worked in a factory but the positions were always short-lived. As soon as she started to get somewhere, the depression would take hold and force her back indoors where she would hide away in her bedroom from the rest of the world. Instead of asking for help, she'd blame me.

'It's all your fault,' she screamed. 'I can't show my face across the door because you're such a little bastard!'

It was partly true, I was fast turning into the 'little bastard' they'd always told me I was but I'd not been born that way, I was just a product of my parents' deep-rooted unhappiness. In a bid to toughen me up, Dad treated me differently to the others. He was stricter but it just caused me to rebel even more.

Once, when I was six, Mum refused to walk us to school. Instead, she told my sister Clair to take me. We were halfway there but, as usual, my mind was miles away thinking of other things when I stepped out into the road without looking. I can still recall the impact of metal against skin and bone as I went sailing up over the car bonnet. My arms and legs splayed out, falling against thin air until I landed with a crashing thud onto the pavement below. The tarmac road juddered against my body causing my bones to rattle inside. I heard Clair's piercing scream: she was hysterical with fear. Someone scooped me up and took me into a nearby house where they laid me on the sofa. I was battered, bruised and a little shocked but I lifted myself up to check on my feet. I gulped when I realised they were bare.

'My trainers,' I cried. I knew I'd be in trouble for losing them.

A man went outside to look, whilst Clair stood tear-stained in the doorway. Moments later a he came back but he only had one trainer in his hand.

'Mum's going to kill me,' I sobbed to Clair, who just cried even more.

The couple stared at us as if we were both mad. Shortly afterwards they took me home. Mum went through the motions of acting like a concerned parent but as soon as the door closed she turned on me.

'Where's your shoe?'

'I lost it,' I trembled, still shaking from the accident.

'Well,' she said, 'wait till your dad hears about it, he won't be happy.'

Most kids would expect love or even a cuddle but I didn't get either. Instead, when Dad got in from work, I was punished for being knocked over as though it was my fault. This was my life, like it or lump it. Dad was right, I had to toughen up and become a man, especially if I wanted to survive my childhood.

Once I got so fed up that I ran away. I was only nine, but like the kitten that had gone before me I saw my chance, took to my heels and made a break for freedom. With nowhere to go, I slept under a hedge in the icy cold. It was a miracle I didn't freeze to death but fortunately that didn't happen. The following morning, I was found and taken back home where I was punished for running off. But it didn't stop me. Not long afterwards, I was messing around with some mates from school. We'd dawdled all the way home and I hadn't realised the time – I was over an hour late. I panicked and ran away again. That evening I slept in a friend's garage without his parents' knowledge. When I finally returned home all hell was let loose.

'You little bastard,' Mum shouted as soon as I came in through the back door. 'Where the hell have you been? Tony, Tony, he's back!' she hollered upstairs to Dad.

Moments later, he was there staring down at me. He told me I was a 'fucking disgrace', a 'fucking little bastard'. I blinked back as he called me everything from a cat to the dog. I took my punishment but vowed to leave home as soon as I was old enough.

By the age of eleven, I was an accomplished thief. I was the artful dodger of Bristol and I'd hang around the corner shop, stealing what I could. One day, I stole two oranges. Fresh fruit always smelled so good that I couldn't resist, but the oranges were large and awkward to hide. As soon as I slipped them into my pockets, you could see the round outline bulging out. The shopkeeper noticed and chased after me down the street.

'Come here, you little sod,' he huffed and puffed behind me.

He was a big fella, but to my amazement he caught me up and gave me a firm and well-aimed clip around the ear. I begged him not to tell my parents and, to his credit, he never did but I was barred from his shop after that. Still I didn't stop. I went from stealing comics and sweets at school, to taking dinner money from other kids' drawers. I never had anything so I needed money to buy nice things, so I could be just like everyone else. Inevitably, I was caught by my teacher and punished. I was on a slippery slope.

I'd been told all my life how useless I was and now I started to believe it. I thought my future was already mapped out and nothing or no one could change it, so what was the point? I was the shadow on the house and our home cast darkness across the entire neighbourhood.

Although Dad worked all the hours God sent, we never had a pot to piss in. Even the milk we poured on our cornflakes was watered down to leave enough for the adults and their precious cups of tea.

I started to resent my friends with their nice houses, loving parents and fresh food on the table. I wanted Mum to look like all the others, to wear nice clothes and to look after us, but she rarely ventured beyond four walls. Instead of love, Mum used her unhappiness as a weapon to beat me with.

'Carry on like this, and I'll have you put away,' she would threaten.

One summer's evening the air was still and the sun was beaming high up in the sky. A gang of us had been playing a game of fox and hounds in nearby woods when we decided to head back home for a game of football in the street. But as soon as my parents spotted me, they called me inside.

'Bed,' Mum ordered.

'But it's still light outside,' I protested.

'Get upstairs now!' Dad's voice boomed.

It was no good; there was no point in arguing because I knew I'd never win. Instead I threw off my trainers in the hallway and headed up to bed.

The room was stuffy and hot so I opened the window to let in some fresh air and as I did I spotted my friends still playing below on the street. It was so light that it seemed like the middle of the day. I glanced down; some of the kids were younger than me. I scowled at the injustice of it all. I was so angry I decided to hold my very own 'secret' protest. I pushed the window wide open, pulled down my trousers and pissed out of it. It didn't change the world but it certainly made me feel a little better. Unfortunately for me, an old lady who lived a few doors down spotted me. She was a nosy, old bugger and decided this was too good an opportunity to miss.

HOME IS WHERE THE HURT IS

The following night I came home from school and I was just about to fling my schoolbag on the floor, when I felt a sharp smack to the side of my head.

'You dirty little bastard!' Mum scolded. The nosy old neighbour had told her everything.

'You're going to be the death of me, I swear,' she cried. She shot me a look of pure disgust and headed back into the front room.

I should've felt ashamed but I wasn't. Instead I wore my new 'tough' image like a badge of honour. When I acted the fool at school or fought back, no one bothered me. I was the nutty boy who lived in the strange house, the lad they called smelly but only behind his back because now I was someone you didn't mess with. My bad lad reputation preceded me. I didn't realise it then, but I was well and truly on the road to ruin.

CHAPTER THREE

The Artful Dodger

B Y THE TIME I was 11, I was totally out of control. Angry and unloved, I wanted to take on the world. My life was ironic because whilst I was heavily disciplined at home, at school I seemed to have a free rein and nothing or no one frightened me.

On my first day at secondary school I saw my chance to stake my claim as the new 'hard kid'. The bike shed was high enough – about six feet tall – but low enough for a small kid like me to shin up onto. The first bell of the day hadn't even rung. I'd only been there a matter of minutes when, egged on by a group of mates from my old junior school, I put one foot on the metal support and lifted myself up onto the corrugated iron roof. I was like a monkey, I'd climb anything.

'Look at me,' I said stretching my arms out to balance myself.

The roof was fixed at an angle, one false move and I'd be

on my back on the floor. I strode around on top of it as if I was king of the world. My mates were standing below and cheered me on. New kids from different intake schools were still arriving and they glanced up at me with their mouths agog. The bike shed was situated right next to the main entrance so, as everyone turned to look up, I felt good. However, my display was short-lived.

'You boy, get down from there right now!'

A car had pulled up below and a stern-looking woman with a severe haircut was sitting behind the steering wheel staring straight up at me. She was probably only in her thirties, but to an 11-year-old boy, she looked ancient. She had pointy, sharp features and scowled as she spoke. But she looked so small and insignificant down there in her car that it made me laugh out loud. It was as if by height alone, I had all the power. However, my mates knew better, they started to shrink back as soon as they saw her but they were still laughing. It was all the encouragement I needed to continue with my one-man protest.

'I said get down from there right now!' she shouted again.

She'd got herself into such a tizz that her face had flushed a deep crimson. A few of the kids pulled faces behind her back. It was the green light I needed.

'What?' I called down to her, like the little sod I was. 'I can't hear you.' I cupped a hand against my ear and pretended to be deaf.

'You heard me alright. Now what's your name? You get down from there this instant because I'm reporting you to the head.'

I looked down at her and sneered.

'Aw, fuck off you old bag.'

Eyes widened beneath me and mouths fell open, I'd just told one of the teachers to fuck off. I'd overstepped the mark, even I knew that. I'd marked my own card but still I refused to budge. By now, my mates Andy and Wayne were killing themselves laughing. I saw them and laughed too. Their response was fuel to me. I had a chip on my shoulder and I saw it as my role in life to be a little sod. I'd behaved so badly through junior school that the teachers had warned me that secondary school would sort me out, but now I was here I was ready to take them all on and this silly woman would be my first victim.

'You're in big trouble,' she warned as she turned away and drove off in search of help.

'Yeah,' I cheered, punching the air. My mates slapped me on the back as I climbed down. I'd been there for fewer than 10 minutes but the Tovey name had already gone down in school legend.

Moments later, the morning bell sounded and I made my way to my new classroom. A few of the older lads patted me on the back as I passed, but my glory was short-lived. Just after register, the classroom door swung open and there she was, the same teacher, only this time she was standing there with the head of year and another bloke.

'That's him, that's the boy I was telling you about,' she crowed with her arms folded across her pinched little chest.

She held my gaze defiantly; she'd won, for now. I looked around at my classmates who were wondering what I'd do next. Before I'd had chance to think, I was dragged unceremoniously out of my chair and through the door as the rest of the class looked on in disbelief. I turned to face my mates and winked. A wide grin spread across my face to let them know that it was okay, normal service had been resumed. A few cheered but they were soon silenced by our new form teacher. I was dragged to the head of year's office, a man called Mr Rawling, who caned me across the bum. Thankfully, I got to keep my trousers up but it still hurt. It was to be the first of many punishments. Days later, I was back again, this time for smoking – a habit I'd developed at the tender age of nine. As a nipper I'd nick any single fags my parents had left on the side then I'd hide in the garden and smoke them in between the bushes and long grass. It was so overgrown that I'd hide just feet from the back door. Sometimes, I'd buy cigs from the local shop where I'd lie, saying they were for Mum or Dad. Back then, shopkeepers didn't ask too many questions, they just took your money. So, I was caned for smoking. Then I was punished for cheeking off a teacher, fighting and even talking in class. I had a reputation and within days of arriving, mine was the name on every teacher's lips. If there was trouble, then Tovey was bound to be involved. Sometimes I wasn't but it didn't matter, my reputation went before me.

One day, I overheard one of the older kids call our teacher a prostitute just because she wore an ankle bracelet. I took it as gospel and imparted this juicy piece of gossip to my mate Andy, who was sitting beside me in class. Unfortunately, the teacher in question had ears like a bat and heard every single word. I was given detention and so was Andy, just for being there. It had been funny at the time but now, sat behind in class, the joke was on me. Andy started to panic. He had to get home, he lived five miles away and had to catch a bus but now he'd miss it, all because of me. Andy knew his parents would worry. I felt a tinge of jealousy; I wished my parents were more like Andy's.

As the clock ticked by, Andy fretted more and more. I could tell he was worried because small beads of sweat had gathered along his brow. He also checked his watch every few seconds, knowing that if he missed this bus then there wouldn't be another one for ages.

'Just leave,' I said watching him. He was becoming more uncomfortable by the minute and I just didn't get it.

What was he was frightened of? Why didn't he just get up and leave? We weren't locked in prison.

But I didn't think like a normal kid because I wasn't 'normal'. I was out of control and I had no boundaries.

'No John, no way,' Andy whispered back to me.

The teacher turned and gave us a look that said 'keep quiet'. The silver bracelet caught the light and twinkled against her ankle. I realised that I had been wrong. She didn't look like a prostitute at all; in fact she looked quite fit. She put a finger to her lips and ordered us to get on with our work.

'Just go!' I whispered to Andy again.

He was getting more stressed by the minute. He shook his head, terrified of getting into more trouble.

'Right,' I said standing up, 'watch this.'

The legs of my chair scraped against the floor causing the teacher to turn around.

'John Tovey where do you think you're going?'

It was a stupid question.

'Home,' I said slamming my book shut.

'Oh no, you're not.'

She put the chalkboard duster down on the side.

'Just watch me,' I replied as I swaggered out of the classroom and slammed the door behind me. I could see

Andy through the glass panel in the door: the look on his face was priceless.

The following morning I received another caning in Mr Rawling's office. By now, I think he was getting sick of seeing both my face and my arse. He was a nice enough bloke but tall, with big hands. His hands put the fear of God into other kids, but not me. Each time he'd whip his cane a little harder waiting for me to cry out with pain but I never did. In truth, it hurt like hell but I'd been brought up to be a man and crying was for wimps.

A few days later, I was back to my usual bad form. When a teacher caught me smoking behind a bus shelter next to the shops, he ordered me to put it out.

'Why?' I replied, holding my hands out in protest, 'I haven't finished it yet.'

Despite my bad boy behaviour, Andy and I were inseparable. Andy was a nice lad who came from a loving home but I was a bad influence. I never told him but I was secretly jealous of his perfect life. Each night he went back to a house where there wasn't any shouting, rows or even raised voices. A home where dinner was always freshly prepared and waiting for him, piping hot on the table. I dreamed of being Andy. On a few occasions he invited me back to his house. The more I went, the more I wanted to stay. His mum and dad were lovely and didn't bat an eyelid when they saw him dragging me through the front door. I loved it at Andy's, it was one of the few places I felt safe, secure and welcome.

Every time I went home, I blamed myself. Maybe I deserved my shit life? Maybe it was because I wasn't a nice kid, that's why I lived in a smelly, dirty house with arguments and rubbish piled high in the garden.

Six months after starting secondary school I decided to bunk off. I didn't think the teachers would care if I wasn't there. It'd probably give them a break from me: God knows they deserved one, especially poor Mr Rawlings whose cane was close to snapping point!

Every day I walked six miles to school and back because there was never money for bus fare. I was so used to walking that it soon became a way of life. I could walk for miles without even batting an eyelid. I was on my way to school one morning when I decided to give myself the day off because I reckoned I'd earned it. I took a picturesque detour through the countryside by the river. I hadn't particularly planned it, I just couldn't face school.

I thrust a hand deep down inside my jacket pocket and grinned when I felt a chocolate bar with my fingers. I'd nicked it the previous day from a shop. Sweets were a luxury and by now I was stealing all the time. As the chocolate melted in my mouth, I contemplated my next move. There'd been talk at school about some older lads who were into something called glue sniffing. I'd heard if you got hold of the right glue, you could get a buzz off it. Armed with very little information, I finished off my chocolate and headed into the nearby town and towards the hardware shop.

Back then, no one had heard of glue sniffing so the shop-keeper kept his stock on wire display units outside the store. I hung around for a bit and, when I was sure no one was looking, I whipped a tin and hid it under my jacket. I strolled back down towards the river, far away from the crowds and placed the tin on the grass and that's when I realised I didn't have a screwdriver to open it with. I scratched my head and looked around.

What good was a tin of glue if I couldn't get the bloody lid off?

I scoured the area until I found a sharp, strong stick, which I managed to wedge underneath the lip of the lid. Slowly but surely, I worked it all the way around until the lid popped off. But I still wasn't sure what I needed to do. I held my face over the brown, gloopy glue and inhaled. My eyes smarted a little but other than a headache, I didn't really feel any different. Something was missing but I didn't know what it was. I tried it a few more times with the lid half on, half off so I could inhale more of the vapour. Finally, after a few attempts, my head began to buzz. That night when I left to go back home I hid the glue in a bush beside the river so I could use it the next time. I expected some flak for having not gone to school but the teachers hadn't called home. I'd got away with it, for now. The following morning I ran into school to try and find some of the older lads.

'I knocked off yesterday and did some of that glue sniffing,' I announced proudly.

'Oh, yeah, and what did you do?' one said turning towards me.

'Well, I took the lid off and sniffed it.'

They all fell about laughing.

'No, you little prick! You've done it wrong, you need to put it into a plastic bag and breathe it in like this,' a lad said holding his hands up to demonstrate.

I felt stupid but I was determined to give it another go. A few days later I was back at the river, this time with a plastic bag in my hand. I did as they said, and almost immediately my eyes rolled back in my skull. The hit I got off it was like being punched in the face. After a while I began to hallucinate. I saw people who weren't really there. My eyes blurred with funny colours – trees became pink instead of green. The more I looked, the more I saw. At one point I spotted the devil sat in a tree opposite me, but I wasn't scared, I was blown away. My mind continued to play tricks on me. Suddenly, a massive hole opened up in the ground by my feet. I jumped up and stood there, teetering on the edge, looking down into the abyss. Then a spaceship appeared and landed right in front of me. I tentatively took a step towards it and climbed on board. I stood on the top of it looking down at this strange and alien land that my head had created. Suddenly, I fainted. When I finally woke up, I was freezing cold and my clothes were soaking wet. I'd passed out right next to the river. It had started to drizzle and I was soaked to the skin. I must have cut a pathetic sight, a young lad, alone and out of school, sniffing glue to pass the time. I convinced myself that I was a hard man but really, I was a frightened little boy. Thinking back now, it makes me shudder. I was 12 years old, getting high and blacking out next to a flowing river; I was a disaster waiting to happen. It's a miracle I'm still alive to tell the tale.

Soon, glue sniffing became the norm. However, the shop-keeper started to get suspicious and I knew my days of nicking from his store were numbered. Instead, I went on the prowl, searching for other stuff to steal. One day I hit the jackpot. Undetected, I sneaked into an unlocked garage that, to my delight, was stacked full with crates of light ale. It was like finding a treasure chest in a secret cave. After that, I'd nip back regularly and help myself to a couple of tins. But I found that the more I drank, the more I needed to get rat-arsed. Soon I was taking four tins at a time. The alcohol made me dizzy but I sat and drank it down by the river. The owners never missed it because they had so much. Instead, I took advantage and treated it like an open bar.

Spending so much time on my own soon became boring so I persuaded my brother Anthony to come with me. Anthony was still at junior school and a little apprehensive about bunking off.

'I'm… I'm not sure,' he stammered.

'Come on, don't be such a wimp, we'll have fun!'

Anthony came with me a few times after that. We shared a can of light ale but he didn't like the taste. Then again, neither did I, it was just an escape from the trouble at home and school. However, it wasn't long before he got cold feet.

'I can't come today, I want to go to school,' he told me looking down at the ground a little embarrassed.

'Right, that's that then,' I huffed.

'It's just that if Dad finds out, he'll kill me…and you!' Anthony insisted, his eyes wide with fear.

He was right of course. Dad would have gone mental. Anthony was younger than me so it wasn't fair to drag him into this, not that Dad would've punished him anyway – Anthony was the apple of his eye; I'd just get it twice as much in the neck for leading my little brother astray.

The following day I was back on my own again. With my classmates safely tucked up in school, I went out on the prowl looking for more stuff to steal. I wandered down a street in a nearby village and that's when I spotted a full bottle of sherry tucked on the passenger seat of a parked car. Thankfully, it was a warm day and the window was half open. I bunched up the sleeve of my shirt and threaded a skinny arm through the gap. I grasped the neck of the bottle between my fingertips and pulled. The window was open just enough to pull the base of the bottle through and then it was mine!

Armed with my new stash of booze, I wandered down to the riverbank where I drank the lot. I soon found sherry didn't agree with me when I threw up, eventually falling into a deep sleep. A passing rambler found me and took me home where I was still so drunk that I didn't even feel the pain from the hiding I got, well, not until the following morning when I'd sobered up anyway. After that, my school attendance was more closely monitored.

'If you don't go to school, they'll come and take you away,' Mum threatened, 'and I'll let them.' But, I didn't believe her. She always said that and nothing ever happened. Instead I let her words wash over me like water off a duck's back.

Still, for a short time I kept my head down and went to school like a good boy but in truth I was bored out of my skull. One afternoon I was sat in a particularly humdrum music lesson when I felt the urge to go to the toilet. I stuck my hand up.

'Yes, John,' the teacher asked.

'Can I go to the toilet?'

The teacher eyed me suspiciously, she didn't believe me because she knew all about my wanderlust and was having none of it.

'No John, you cannot,' she said simply before turning back to address the rest of the class. A few of them sniggered, which wound me up even more.

'But,' I said, interrupting her. 'I'm bursting! I need the toilet. I need a piss!' I repeated cheekily.

My mates started to laugh because they didn't believe me either.

'I said no, John.'

It was too late, my bladder was at bursting point and I was worried I'd piss my pants right there and then.

'I need to go,' I begged.

The teacher slammed her book down on the desk to make a point.

'John Tovey are you deaf? I said NO!'

I hated her and everyone knew. The rest of the class turned away from her and back to me as if watching a game of tennis. The ball was in my court and it was my shot next.

'I'm not messing about. I need to go and I need to go *now*.' I demanded.

The class turned back towards the teacher.

'Well, you should have thought about that before the lesson. Besides, if I let you out of my class how do I know you won't just walk out of school like you've done before? Hmm?' she said raising an eyebrow.

'That's it,' I cried, getting to my feet. I cupped a hand over my genitals to try and stop the flow. 'I can't wait any longer!'

I ran over to the large black bin in the corner of the room, unzipped my trousers and pissed in it. The relief was so wonderful that I didn't hear the uproar behind me. The whole class had gone into meltdown. The nutty boy had done it again and, even by my standards, this was pretty bad. I zipped up my trousers and turned back just in time for the teacher to hand me a folded note.

'Here,' she said thrusting it into my hand before wiping hers against her skirt as if I had a disease. 'Take this to the head. It explains what you've just done, you disgusting little boy. You're going to be in so much trouble.'

I looked down at the pathetic piece of paper and crumpled

it into a ball in my fist. I was in enough trouble so I threw it on the ground and stormed out of the classroom towards the main exit. As luck would have it, the next person walking towards me in the corridor was the teacher's son. He was a whole school year above me and probably didn't even know who I was, but I knew him and that was enough. I balled my hand into a fist and leapt on him, punching him square in the face. I didn't stop to check or turn back instead; I ran out of the school and even banged on a few classroom windows as I passed. Faces crowded against glass to get a better look, cheering me on as I sprinted towards the school gate. I felt superhuman. I wasn't frightened and now I was in complete meltdown.

With nowhere to go I headed for my favourite spot down by the river. Unbeknown to me the school had called my parents and alerted the police who were out searching for me. Later that evening I got an almighty telling off and, when I returned to school the following day, I felt guilty when I saw the state of my poor victim. His eye was purple and swollen to twice its normal size. I'd given him a right old shiner all because of who his mum was. To his credit, it took him a few weeks before he finally buckled and told the head who'd really hit him. As soon as they knew it was me, all hell broke loose and I was given the cane again and another hiding back at home.

A few hours later, I was in the front room when I heard someone knock at the door. It was a social worker and she'd come to speak to mum and dad. Her name was Mrs Savage and it suited her and her occupation. I knew it was serious when they sent me upstairs to my bedroom so they could talk about me. I heard my name mentioned lots of time along with the words 'trouble' and 'out of control'.

An hour later I was called back downstairs because Mrs Savage wanted to speak to me.

'John, you've got to go to a new school. It's all been arranged. I've just been discussing it with your mum and dad, who also think it's for the best.'

I took a sharp intake of breath. This was it, it was finally happening. I was frightened because I realised that I didn't want to go to another school, I wanted to stay here with my mates.

'B... but,' I began

'It's all sorted,' Mum snapped, shutting me up. She took a drag of her fag and turned towards the social worker.

'What kind of school? Where is it?' I asked Mrs Savage, but she'd stopped listening and had turned back to my parents.

'So, I'll be in touch. In the meantime I'll make all the necessary arrangements.'

But I wanted to know where I was going and how long for. After she'd left, Mum grabbed me by the arm.

'See, I warned you,' she hissed. 'I told you they'd send you away and now it's finally happened. I hope you're pleased with yourself. It's all your fault.'

And she was right, it was.

CHAPTER FOUR

Nutty Boy

'RIGHT, YOU LITTLE bastard, off to bed because they're coming for you tomorrow, you're getting put away,' Mum announced late one Sunday evening.

I'd not been at school since the expulsion for hitting the teacher's son but no one had said anything about going away, only Mum, and I'd never believed her. I thought back to the social worker's visit a few weeks before and my heart sank.

'Where am I going?' I asked, begging Mum for more information.

'You're getting put away just like I said.'

She turned and took another drag from her fag. The embers burned bright orange as her mouth puckered. Her leathery cheeks looked like a deflated balloon as she sucked the life out of the cig between her fingers. I watched glumly as it withered and died away. I sat and waited for more information but Mum turned back towards the TV. She crushed the fag butt down into the ashtray and stubbed it out. That was all I was getting. Inside I was petrified but I didn't want to give her the satisfaction of knowing. I got up to leave the room and as I did she called to me.

'They're picking you up at 8.30am sharp!'

She'd already packed a bag for me – a light blue 1950s style suitcase that looked as old and battered as everything else we owned.

That night I couldn't sleep, my dreams were haunted by strange men in dark suits coming to get me. They had chains and jangly keys dangling from silver loops on their belts. I gasped and sat bolt upright in bed. My vest was sodden with sweat and sticking to my skin – the boy who feared nothing was frightened. I'd brought it on myself, I knew that much. I'd been a cocky little sod yet, despite all my bravado, I never believed Mum's threats would come true, but now they had and now I was about to be sent away. I was 12 years old and, for the first time in my life, I felt vulnerable. Little did I know that things were about to get a whole lot worse.

The following morning a cab pulled up outside our house.

'Taxi's here,' Mum hollered.

Dad had already left for work, he hadn't even bothered to say goodbye. My sisters and brother had left for school but no one had said a word. I wondered if they'd even been told. It made me feel worse. Inwardly I was shaking but I knew there was no point arguing, it wouldn't do any good. I waited for Mum to hug or kiss me but she just stuck out an arm and handed me my suitcase. She didn't look upset – she barely even looked at me. With her other arm she opened up the door and shooed me out.

'Bye then,' I muttered turning back in the hope she'd

change her mind. She gave me one last withering look and slammed the door. I was all alone. Hitching up the case, I struggled over towards the cab. The suitcase was bulky and heavy so the driver got out and put it in the boot.

'Thanks,' I muttered miserably, climbing onto the back seat.

As the car slowly wound its way out of our road and towards Bristol city centre I tried to console myself.

Maybe it'd be an adventure?

I was a little sod but I was also an eternal optimist.

After half an hour we pulled up outside a building where I was herded along with half a dozen other kids onto a waiting minibus. I was stunned when I saw two girls standing in the queue. I didn't think there would be girls.

Maybe it wouldn't be so bad after all?

I found out that we were being taken to a naughty kids' school in Minehead for children like me, who had what society called 'challenging behaviour'. I sneaked a sly look at the others as we climbed on board. One by one our names were checked off a list on a clipboard. I took my seat and glanced around. They were all teenagers and at least three years older than me.

'Oi, what you looking at you little shit?' a tough-looking kid called from the back seat.

I tried to ignore him but he continued.

'Do you smoke? Got any fags?'

I shook my head. I'd thought about nicking a few from home but decided against it because I thought we'd be searched. Now I wish I had because they all had them. I spotted them exchanging furtive glances, I saw cigarettes stuffed up sleeves and felt envious.

God, I could murder a fag right now, I thought bitterly to myself.

Moments later, I was budged along the seat by a fat lad who had squashed in next to me. He looked over, wanting me to move up but I was hemmed in and didn't have anywhere left to go. He was older and his arse took up more than his fair share of seat. I ignored him and stared hard out of the window. It had just started to drizzle with rain and it was beginning to patter softly against the glass. The man with the clipboard called out the last name and climbed in. Someone shut the door and the minibus spluttered into life. We were all thrown backwards as the bus juddered off and along the road. As we made our way out of Bristol, the lad on the back seat shuffled closer towards the window. It was an old-fashioned vehicle and the back window had a weird kind of fishtail contraption which opened outwards.

'Perfect,' he laughed as he cupped his hands around a cig, struck a match and lit it.

He took a drag and blew the grey smoke out of the side of his mouth and through the open window. I looked towards the front, half-expecting the man with the clipboard to say something but he didn't care. Within minutes, someone else had lit up. You could smell it in the air. Soon, they were all at it but no one, not even the driver, said a word. He probably knew better than to take on a load of kids like us. Although the window was open, soon the air was thick with cigarette smoke. It made me crave a fag even more. We'd only been going a short while then the hard lad dipped forward and tapped me on the back.

'Here you go,' he whispered pushing something into my fingertips; it was a half smoked fag.

It felt hot against my skin but I turned my hand away and hid it up my sleeve being careful not to singe my wrist. I took a drag and tried to blow the smoke backwards towards the open window. The hard lad caught my eye and grinned. I smiled back and immediately began to feel better. I realised just how insignificant I was. I'd been tough at my previous school but sat here right now, I was way out of my depth. Suddenly, the fat lad next to me started up a conversation.

'So, what you in for?' he asked as if we were on our way to prison.

'Fighting, but mainly for hitting the teacher's son,' I replied. There was no need to lie, I was enough of a little shit as it was.

The lad smirked and shook his head in disbelief. It gave me confidence.

Maybe these kids weren't so bad after all?

I started to laugh.

'I also pissed in a bin.' I boasted. 'You should've seen the teacher's face, she was well pissed off.'

The lad at the back began to laugh and soon the whole bus had joined in: it felt good to be holding court again. Through the laughter I noticed a girl sat on the opposite side to me. She was the only one not laughing. She was pretty and slim, with dark hair, and I was desperate to impress her. She was wearing a cool black jacket with a target on the back.

If she were a bloke, I'd wanna hit her because of that target, I thought randomly.

But she wasn't a bloke and I never, ever hit women.

'What's your name?' I asked.

A huge jeer erupted from the back of the bus and I flushed bright red, but I refused to give up. The girl looked over at me with disdain and out of the window again. The lad next to me saw and snorted with laughter.

'How old are you then?' I said, trying again.

'Fourteen,' she sniffed.

Ah, an older woman, just what I needed.

But she made it clear she wasn't interested in me. Instead, she shifted in her seat and turned away.

'Aww, don't be like that. He's only a baby,' a voice from the back of the bus called.

I shrugged and laughed along. I was still a kid so I was used to women ignoring me. But the lads were more vocal and soon I knew what each and every one of them was 'in' for – nicking mostly, especially from shops. But these weren't the sort of kids who went to Woolworths to steal a packet of sweets; they were professional shoplifters who'd steal anything that wasn't nailed down.

The countryside whizzed by in a rain-soaked blur outside. I watched as droplets of rain streaked across the glass. Soon motorway gave way to dual carriageways and then one long, dreary country road – one road in, one road out.

Where the hell was this place?

We'd been travelling for around two hours when the minibus finally pulled up. The building was Victorian, but looked grand with a big wooden doorway, a courtyard made of cobbled stone and a long gravel drive. It all seemed very classy and not at all what I'd been expecting. The high roof was covered with grey slate and, as soon as I clocked it, I knew it wouldn't be long before I'd be up there, running around and acting the fool. I was right and by the end of the week, I'd got my wish.

The other kids were just as disruptive and had been expelled or excluded from their previous schools. Some had been chucked out for fighting, some for much worse although I didn't stop to ask too many questions. It was a mixed school with 11 being the youngest and 16 being the oldest.

Once the minibus had parked up we unloaded our suitcases and filed through to the school canteen. Lunch was waiting for us and I was ready for it. With very little to eat at home and a long journey behind me, I was absolutely starving. However, what I didn't expect was the total array of choice on offer. Back at home everything either came from a packet or a tin but here there were dozens of hot meals to choose from, all served up with mashed potatoes, chips, roasties and fresh veg. There were also jugs of fresh orange juice, fizzy drinks and even milkshakes! I was astounded; I thought you only got posh grub like this in a hotel. I greedily grabbed a plate of pie, chips and gravy and sat down at one of the tables. I went up for second helpings and then thirds. There was no stopping me. I was so busy tucking in that I didn't notice a group of lads approach from behind.

"'Ere, kid. What you in for then?"

I didn't want any trouble but I also didn't want to look like a pushover.

'Fighting,' I shrugged without looking up.

My hair was long and down to my shoulders and I was wearing flared green trousers – I stood out like a sore thumb. I lifted up my head from my food and gulped as I took them in. These were skinhead lads. They looked cool but intimidating dressed in their tight jeans, braces, Doc Marten boots and crisp Fred Perry tops.

'Ooh, fighting,' one of them cooed. 'What? With girly hair?' he said twirling a lock of my hair around his index finger. I was terrified he'd beat me up so I kept quiet.

The others laughed but thankfully, that's all they did. I sighed with relief when they finally walked away. I'd always been wary of skinheads and punks. To a kid my age, they were absolutely terrifying. But I knew if I wanted to survive then these were exactly the type of people I needed to get in with.

Just then the canteen door swung open and a group of girls wandered in chatting. A couple of them were swearing, whilst another twisted chewing gum around her finger before popping it back inside her mouth. I grinned, things were looking up! Suddenly I remembered my collar-length hair and crouched down, trying to hide. I looked like a right prat compared to the other cool lads. What girl would ever look at me dressed like this?

An hour later, I was herded along the corridor to a dormitory that I was told I would be sharing with six others. Everyone was older than me but we all had to share bunk beds. At teatime, a man walked in wheeling a trolley of something – medication. For some reason, lots of kids suffered from asthma so he dished out various inhalers. I didn't need one so instead, he handed me a pile of folded up clothes. As soon as I saw them my heart sank.

Second hand clothes again.

But, unlike the ones back at home, at least these ones were clean.

The conversation followed along the same lines as it did on the minibus. When I told the others in my dorm that I was in for fighting they laughed. I was puzzled until I caught them looking at my puny body. I was a late developer, small and hairless, but unbeknown to them, I could still pack a punch.

The following morning, when a skinhead lad asked me what sort of music I was into I answered honestly.

'Abba.'

It was social suicide.

He inhaled a sharp intake of breath.

'Fucking Abba!' he screamed.

'Hey Gibsy,' he said beckoning to his mate in disbelief. 'This kid likes fucking Abba!'

The pair of them burst out laughing and again I felt like a complete prat. At first I thought I was going to get my head kicked but the more they laughed, the safer I felt: these were older skinheads, they just wanted to take the mickey out of me.

'Aw, stop it Brownie, I'm gonna piss myself!' Gibsy begged, slapping his mate on the back.

'Yeah, but look at his hair,' Brownie sniggered. 'He looks like a bleeding hippy!'

They exploded again as I stared down at the ground trying hard to think of something clever to say.

'Yeah,' I said a little too defensively. 'It's only 'cos I can't afford to get it cut.'

The skinheads looked over at each other and howled once more.

'Aww, is that why you grow it like a girl?' Gibsy whined.

I felt stupid. I didn't want to look like this and, although I hated my jumble sale clothes, it had never mattered before but now it did.

'Hey, tell you what,' I said, my eyes firing with excitement, 'how about one of you shave it all off for me?'

They stopped laughing, stood up straight and faced me. That'd got their attention.

'What? Like a proper little skinhead?' Gibsy said.

'Yeah,' I nodded.

I was sick of being the smelly kid, the one who everyone laughed at. But now, right here I could do something about it and my parents weren't here to stop me. I was going to be a skinhead and, for the first time in my life I was going to be cool. That day, Gibsy and Brownie took a pair of clippers to my girly hair and shaved the lot off – grade one. I liked the feel of the stubble under my fingers. I felt clean and revived but, most of all, I knew I had the respect of the older skinheads.

One of the lads looked down at my clothes with pity; my flared trousers looked even more ridiculous now I had no hair. He disappeared but minutes later he returned and threw me a pair of old jeans.

'Here kid, take these.'

I grabbed them gratefully.

Later that day, I was given something I'd never had in my life before: pocket money. With a whole pound in my hand, I felt like the richest man on earth. Determined to fit in with my new set of friends, I went down to Minehead where I found a backstreet jewellers that offered ear piercing for just 50p. I knew it would use up half my money, but I didn't care. The older lads wore a stud in one ear and I wanted to be just like them. I handed my money over. But for 50p, the service was pretty basic. There was no piercing gun, instead, a big bloke with hands the size of shovels, pushed a sterilised needle through my earlobe. It hurt like hell and I winced as he dabbed at it with cotton wool, popped in a silver-coloured stud and sent me on my way. My transformation was complete.

Unlike my old secondary school, here I had lots of freedom. It was an improvement school – we were classed as 'unruly' children. There were 50 of us in total: 25 boys and 25 girls. Although the building was meant to contain and help rehabilitate our behaviour, the doors were never locked. Most days we'd just walk straight out of the front door. We had the freedom to come and go as we pleased and because it was late summer and the nights were still light, as long as we were back by 8.30pm, no one batted an eyelid. I tagged along with the older skins. We walked into Minehead and headed straight to the beach to kill time. Older people and young families cleared the path when they saw us coming with our uniform of shaved heads, tight jeans and threatening Doc Marten boots. Skinheads had a bad reputation back then but I liked the respect we got from others. I was only a baby though and I didn't realise that this so-called 'respect' was actually fear.

One day, we walked into one of the many arcades littered along the seafront. It was busy and crammed full of holiday-makers. The sound of buzzers and bells was so deafening that the staff didn't notice us nudging machines trying to get money out of them. We nudged them so hard that we set the alarms off. The owner was furious and threw us out onto the street. After that, we perfected a hammy 'fight' scene where one skinhead would throw another against a machine so hard, it would make all the two pence pieces spill out across the floor. We grabbed what we could and scarpered. I laughed so hard that I felt sick.

Even though I was still a kid, I tagged along with the others so that I could chat up women. We picked on groups of girls, usually holidaymakers dreaming of a holiday romance.

However, most girls' ideal date wasn't a yob from the local naughty boys' school so unsurprisingly, we never had much luck. Most would run a mile when they saw us coming. I think they thought we wanted to beat them up but actually all we wanted to do was kiss them.

But we did beat 'jitters' up. Jitters were what other people called rockers. We looked out for them on the seafront and, once we'd spotted a jitter, we'd pile in with bare fists. We had a few jitters in school and, even though I once had long hair, I was now as bad as the others. I shared the dorm with one jitter but he was so weird that once he set his bed on fire when he was still in it. We all gave him a wide berth after that – the poor lad clearly wasn't right in the head.

Despite our threatening manner we never picked on punks because they were our mates. In fact, a few punks went out with us on our regular seaside jaunts. At night we'd search for cigarette kiosks to smash so we could nick the fags inside. Once I took a house brick and pummelled in the front of a machine. There was glass everywhere but I didn't cut myself because my hands were still small and nimble enough to pull out the single cigarettes inside. Back then, shopkeepers were more trusting and placed the machines outside the front of their stores. My favourite was the one outside Woolworths. It charged 30p for eight single Embassy fags – daylight robbery in my book – so I robbed it back. But, after my third attempt, the manager got wise and moved the bloody thing back indoors.

I discovered that lots of my classmates didn't have parents so they'd never had any kind of authority – it was why they behaved like they did. It was ironic because I'd had too much authority from my parents and it had put me here! But now, being able to do what I wanted felt like being on constant holiday – I'd just been let out of prison, not put in one. Everything was perfect, only one thing was missing: my mates back home.

Every three or four weeks, the kids who did have homes could go back to visit. My friends were a bit shocked when they first saw me with my grade one skinhead. I looked much tougher than they'd remembered but underneath I was still the same old John. Only one person hated my new look and that was Dad.

'You look like a thug,' he barked. Then he spotted my earring and staggered back in horror.

'And as for that,' he said pointing at the offending ear, 'you can get rid of it.'

By now my ear was fully healed so whenever I went home, I'd just take the stud out to keep the peace. When I went out I'd simply slip it in my pocket and pop it back in outside in the street. After a while, I realised the stud was more of a hindrance anyway. Lots of lads had had them ripped out during fights, causing horrific damage to their ears. I didn't want to end up with a deformed ear, so I took it out for good. Even without the earring, I still attracted my fair share of attention from girls who wanted to 'mother' me. With my skinhead haircut, they certainly seemed more interested. One day a girl called Tracy lured me around the back of the school where she pinned me up against the wall and snogged my face off. I loved it! It was my first proper kiss and I felt on top of the world, delighted that someone had fancied me. To make things even better, at 14 years old, Tracy was an older woman!

Shortly afterwards, we were hanging around the common

room when I heard one of the older lads talking about glue sniffing so I butted in.

'I've tried that,' I boasted.

The older skins looked down in disbelief as I recounted my days spent down at the riverbank with the glue, the plastic bags and the passing out.

'You're a little loony,' Brownie smirked.

I grinned. He meant it as a term of affection. After that, 'little loony' became my new nickname. Brownie was the hardest skin I knew and what he said went. There was Gibsy, Ozzy and Dave in the gang, and I looked up to them all. In many ways, I became the butt of their joke but I didn't care. I felt protected and lived up to my new title at every opportunity.

"Ere John, light my fag, will you?" one of the lads asked one day. I dutifully walked over, took out a match and lit the end of his cigarette.

'Good man,' he said patting me on the back.

Not long afterwards, he asked me to light it again only this time in class and in front of the teacher. I wilfully obliged and was later punished. Soon, the requests were becoming more and more ridiculous.

'Go and jump out of that tree,' one lad ordered.

I walked over, climbed up to a high branch, shut my eyes and jumped. The gang loved it and asked me to take more and more risks. Stupidly, I did as they said. I was told to set off the smoke alarms so I blew cigarette smoke directly against the alarm in the common room. The whole building was evacuated but no one knew it was me – it gave me even more confidence. Afterwards, I punched a hole clean through one of the leaded windows in the hallway. Again, I escaped unpunished and now there was no stopping me. I'd regularly punch out the glass just to get a reaction from the other lads.

'Look at the little loony,' they'd chant slapping me on the back in respect. I lapped it up.

Sometimes, when I punched the glass I'd cut my fist but I'd just wrap it in toilet paper to stem the flow. Pain didn't scare me but rejection did.

One day, we were all in the common room but we were bored. A few lads were playing a game of snooker in a corner of the room so, without warning, I walked over, picked up the white ball and threw it straight out of the window, smashing glass everywhere. The whole gang cheered but the snooker lads weren't quite so impressed. They sent me outside and made me get down on my hands and knees in the long grass to look for the ball so they could carry on with their game.

The staff hated my new-found cockiness and soon started to fine me for damages to school property. Every broken pane of glass or misdemeanour earned me a deduction from my weekly pocket money or half a day's community work. At first I took the punishment but it was monotonous work pulling out weeds between the cobbles in the courtyard, so I told them to take my money instead. Without a regular income my debt to the school grew larger by the week and, because I had no money, I went out and nicked what I could.

If I thought I'd done glue sniffing before it was nothing in comparison to now. It was hard-core and highly addictive until soon, I was glue sniffing almost every day. The fumes sent me crazy and I lashed out at staff. Sometimes they'd have to restrain me; if anything I became more of a liability and, instead of my behaviour improving it became ten times worse.

I ran away from school a few times and hitched all the way from Minehead back to Bristol just for the hell of it. I did it partly to prove that I could. Someone from the school drove out to get me back but sometimes they'd catch me on the road. It didn't take much detective work with just one road in and one road out.

'Why do you do it, eh? Why did you run away?' Dad demanded.

His question stumped me for a moment but I appealed to his better nature.

'Because they won't let me watch cricket on TV.' I replied.

Dad shook his head; he didn't have a clue what to do with me. I blamed the cricket, but deep down I knew it was more than that. Even though I wouldn't admit it, I missed my friends. I also missed my sisters, my brother and, in a bizarre way, even my parents. Looking back, I had it far too easy at the new place and, like most things in life, you don't realise what you've lost until it's too late.

One afternoon we were on a break so I wandered along to the common room with a bunch of the lads. A staff member walked into the room carrying a record player. Normally it was kept locked away to stop us from nicking it but today we were allowed to use it as a special privilege.

'Here you go lads.' The youth worker smiled, placing it down on top of a table in a corner of the room. 'Bring your vinyl down and you can play some music.'

A few people disappeared off to their rooms to fetch records. Some carried on playing snooker but I just sat there waiting to see who would bring what down. Minutes later, a lad walked in cradling his albums in his arms as if they were a newborn baby.

'Let's have a look,' a tough kid asked making a grab.

'Get off,' he warned, protecting them.

It was an unwritten rule; you didn't touch anyone's records. He walked over to the record player, slid out an album from its sleeve and gently placed the needle down. Seconds later the room was full of ska music. I opened my ears and mind, the music was amazing! My embarrassing flirtation with Abba became a thing of the past as I realised that this was the way forward. The bands on the front of the albums all looked so cool and the music was infectious. It was different to anything else I'd heard before. As the record ended the lad picked up another, put it on the turntable and turned the volume up loud. There were a few crackles as the sound filtered through the speakers then a man's voice boomed across the room and the music kicked in fast and furious. Everyone started to smile and dance around, kicking out their legs and acting like complete nutters. I was taken aback and wandered over to get a closer look. I sat on the ground and budged in as close as I could to the album cover. It had a crazy bunch of lads lined up on the front like a human train. I wanted to pick it up but was too frightened because I knew I'd get my head kicked in. Instead, I sat, listened and watched the hypnotic effect it had on everyone in the room. In an instant everyone's spirits were lifted. One great track followed another. Not all of them as upbeat as the first. And then it came on, a track called 'Land of Hope and Glory'; it stole my breath away because I identified with every single word. In fact, it was so close to my own life that I wondered if someone had written it about me, a little sod who'd been locked away.

'What's this lot called?' I asked a bloke standing next to the speakers.

'Madness,' he told me.

I smirked: it was an apt name.

'They're brilliant, aren't they?' he grinned back.

I nodded, shut my eyes and let the music wash over me. Soon, we'd listened to the entire album and I begged him to put it on again. And so my lifelong obsession with Madness began – the longest love affair of my life and something that is still on-going to this day. Somehow their music touched me in a way that nothing else could – it had put its hook in me. Afterwards, I nipped down to Minehead to nick what I could – booze, fags and now Madness singles. I stole them from Woolworths. I became so obsessed that one of the lads put their records on a tape for me. I listened to it so much that the tape warped and snapped in half. I was on the cusp of teenagehood and looked upon the band, mainly Suggs and Lee Thompson, as older brothers I never had. They were a handful of years older than me but to a kid stuck in an improvement school in the middle of nowhere, they were gods. I longed to be like them with their snazzy suits and crombies. Before I'd looked up to the skinhead gang but now it was Madness.

When one of the older lads offered to tattoo my arms I let him. It was the eve of my 13th birthday but I knew was being 'marked' as a man. He drew along my arms using a needle and a pot of navy ink. It was smudged and a little amateur but it made me feel older somehow. I watched as he inked some initials into my skin: A.C.A.B.

'What does it mean?' I asked.

'All coppers are bastards,' one of the lads behind me sniggered.

I twisted my arm to get a better look and as I did, I gulped with fear because I knew if he ever saw it, Dad would kill me. Still, it was done now and I felt I belonged even more.

I loved my tattoo but I loved one thing more – football, namely Bristol City. When I was younger, Dad took me to home matches. I'd worn my red and white scarf with pride even though, like everything else, I'd stolen it. I was nine and walking through a caravan site when curiosity got the better of me and I tried one of the doors. To my utter surprise it was unlocked. I popped my head inside and that's when I saw it, a red and white scarf hanging from a hook, just inside the door. My fingers were itching to grab it so I did. When Dad asked me later where I'd got it from I told him I'd found it. I don't think he believed me but he let me keep it all the same. After that, whenever we went to a game, I'd wear my stolen scarf with pride. I loved going to football with Dad because it was the one thing we shared in common. Now, miles away from home, I missed our Saturdays at the home games. Instead, I bored everyone silly with my love of Bristol City.

Bristol City has one main rival and that's Bristol Rovers. It later transpired the headmaster, although not a bad man, was obsessed with Bristol Rovers. He knew I was a die-hard City fan and also the little sod that'd spent the past year wreaking havoc in his school. So, when he called me into his office one warm summer's afternoon, I knew it wasn't for a chat about football.

'I'm afraid you can't come back here next year,' he said looking through a pile of papers on his desk.

I was stunned.

'Why not, what have I done?' I said, getting a little shirty.

'It's more what you haven't done John,' he said, holding his hand up in mid air to stop my protests. 'For example you've been knocking off lessons and that's just the start, you've also been spotted hanging around Minehead causing havoc. We've had reports of violence and you've even lashed out at members of my staff when they've tried to restrain you. To be honest, we just can't handle you here, you're too disruptive.'

'I...' I said beginning to speak but words escaped me. He was right, I was guilty as charged. It seemed I'd been having too much of a good time.

'Anyway, it's been decided,' he continued. 'In September, you will go to another school – somewhere more suited to your, er, behaviour.' He emphasised the last word so slowly it made me cringe.

I went to say something but he refused to listen.

'That is enough,' he said stopping me in mid-flow. 'Close the door on your way out.'

'Bastard Rovers fan,' I spat with venom as I slammed the door behind me.

The school had an end of year disco, I knew it would be my last so I set about trying to snog as many girls as I could. I knew I was going to miss Minehead and my friends. I didn't have a clue where they would send me and, to be honest, I was a little worried. But I had the whole summer in front of me and September felt like a lifetime away.

CHAPTER FIVE

Locked In

SUMMER PASSED BY all too quickly. One day, the same old social worker knocked at the front door to take me to visit my new school. Unusually, Mum and Dad insisted on coming with me. I smelt a rat.

'It'll be great there,' Mum tried to convince me during the journey.

'Yeah,' Dad agreed.

Reassured, I allowed myself to relax but as soon as we arrived I knew it was going to be different from my last school. It was big and posh, but unlike the last place, this one had fences running all the way around it.

'Why are there bars on the windows?' I asked a man who had a huge bunch of keys dangling from his belt. He used them to unlock the gate in front of us.

'This is an approved school John,' the social worker said butting in.

I wasn't sure what an approved school was but I knew I

didn't approve of the bars on the windows and all the security. It was as if they wanted to lock the kids in rather than keep the world out. The social worker was a smart lady and she tried her best to sell it to me. Her words were backed up by the nice headmaster who showed us around.

'You'll love it here,' Mrs Savage gushed. 'A nice room, with lots of boys your own age. You'll make lots of new friends!'

I wasn't sure but I knew I didn't have much say in the matter because the decision had already been made.

Sure enough, like the time before, a minibus picked me and three others up from Bristol and took us to our new school. The other lads on the bus were from the city, just like me, but I didn't know or particularly like them. They were a totally different calibre of nutter and they took drugs. One had a professional tattoo, even though he was only 14. Another one had a homemade tattoo like me, but his was on his face, underneath his eye.

As soon as we entered the building the staff seemed to disappear. Within seconds I was put in a head lock. I gasped and strained my neck to see a rough-looking bloke approach as his mate held me down. He wanted to know how much money I had.

'Nothing!' I pleaded, 'I'm skint.'

But he rifled through my pockets all the same.

As his mate let go I gasped for air and gripped my neck; I felt as if I'd just been strangled.

'You get any money, you to bring it to me, understand?'

I nodded back, too terrified to say no.

Afterwards, I watched my back. There were no girls here just boys. But they weren't ordinary teenagers, these were hardened criminals. You knew, given half a chance, they'd smash a plank of wood over your head just for the fun of it. These were lads who'd come from all over the country. They were so bad that other towns had shipped them out and sent them here – like the last chance saloon.

The headmaster, who had originally shown me around, suddenly reappeared. I smiled when I saw him, relieved to see a friendly face at last, but he just blanked me. It had all been an act. He opened his mouth and started to bellow at the boys in our dormitory and everyone stood to attention like soldiers. I shut my eyes and shuddered – he sounded just like Dad.

I started to realise this was nothing like a school at all; it was a prison. All our movements were monitored and, unlike the old place, the door was always kept firmly locked. There was no chance of bunking off or even slipping out – the locked gates and eight foot high wire-link fence saw to that. It was so bad that we were even locked inside the TV room. Even though I was only 13, I wasn't the youngest. Some were a whole year younger, but most lads were teenagers aged up to 16. There were 40 'pupils' in total. Most of them saw it as a stepping stone to a young offenders institute and ultimately jail. It was a depressing and entirely sobering place to be. Even the atmosphere felt intimidating. I kept my head down and tried to keep out of trouble.

Showers were a particular torture for me. I was still small with a puny, underdeveloped body and despite all my bravado, I was actually a bit of a prude. I don't know why, maybe I saw my clothes, especially my 'skinhead uniform', as cloth armour. Once naked, I felt totally exposed and open to ridicule and my lack of hair, both on my head and down below, made me a prime target.

"Ere look, Tovey's hairless, like a little girl!' a big lad shouted to the others in the shower one morning and then I got a pasting for being a late starter.

Unbelievably, worse was to come. There were two men who worked the night-shift together – perverts, I called them, and I did my best to avoid them. They'd dream up 'punishments' just so they could single out young boys who they'd then sexually abuse. One of these punishments involved getting us all out of bed in the middle of the night, usually because someone was making a noise. Even the slightest sound would be enough to set them off. They'd switch the light on and we'd be ordered from our beds and made to line-up outside, half-naked, whatever the weather. One night, a 13-year-old kid was having a homemade tattoo done by a skinhead in our dorm. The tattoo was taking too long and the skinhead soon lost his patience with it. Without warning, he produced a flick knife and sliced straight into the poor boy's arm making him cry out with pain, his screams reaching fever pitch when the skin poured thick navy ink into the cuts. The staff came running but as usual, it was the fat pervert and his weasel friend on duty. They made us stand in our underpants for an hour outside in the bitter cold. Afterwards, some of the lads got wise and started wearing two pairs of pants so that they didn't freeze their bollocks off. But the men realised and brought in a new 'checking' system. They stopped people indiscriminately to check whether they were wearing two pairs of pants but they always picked on the youngest, including me. All the boys were ordered to line up whilst the men put their hands inside their waistbands – of course, it was all a ruse.

One evening, after almost an hour and a half of standing

half naked in sub-zero temperatures, we were told to queue up inside. I made sure I was near the front because I wanted to get it over and done with. But as I neared the perverts my heart quickened.

'Come here,' the fat bastard called, beckoning me forward. My whole body trembled as I hesitated and took a cautious step towards him.

He roughly pulled the elastic waistband of my underpants away from my stomach. I felt sick but tried to focus on a stain on the wall behind his head. I didn't want him to sense my fear but cringed as he peered down at my underdeveloped and pubeless body. My heart beat fast as I waited to be sent on my way but then he did something else, he snaked a hand deep down into my pants and fondled my genitals. My eyes widened with horror and I looked at him, pleading with him to stop. I was petrified the others would see and call me a poof. But he didn't care; he just grinned and let the elastic ping shut against my stomach. Hot and ashamed, I stole a glance behind me but thankfully, no one had seen. That night I didn't sleep, instead I waited for someone to say something but no one ever did. Being labelled a queer was the worst thing that could happen to you in a place like this but it looked like I was safe, for now.

But not everyone was as lucky. One 15-year-old lad was labelled gay and his life made torture. In the end, things became so desperate that he calmly removed the cord from his dressing gown, looped it over the top of a toilet cubicle and tried to hang himself. Thankfully, he was discovered before he'd managed to do any real harm but as punishment his dressing gown cord was confiscated and he had to wear it without one. Afterwards, he walked around with his arms folded tightly around his waist to keep it shut, but it just served to fire the bullies up even more.

'Hey, look everyone, here comes flasher,' a lad taunted as the boy walked inside the dorm one evening.

I cringed because he'd suffered enough, but after that day, 'flasher' became his new nickname. I sympathised with him but I was also too scared to get involved because life was hard enough. I was just grateful it wasn't me.

Bullying was so rife that another 13-year-old lad was badly burned after he tried to set fire to his bed in a suicide attempt. Instead of sympathy, the others mocked him when he finally returned with badly burned hands back to the dorm.

'Fucking attention seeker,' someone jeered and they all joined in.

'Fucking loser,' another called.

'Mummy's boy.'

Soon he was bullied for being an attention seeker, all because the poor kid had tried to commit suicide. It was horrendous.

There were three dormitories situated on the main landing, each fitted out with bunk beds. One dormitory held 12–15 boys, and the perverts would take it in turns to pick out a particular dorm for punishment. As younger lads, more than often, we'd be chosen. The fondling incident wasn't a one-off, it happened a few times but I was far too frightened to report it. I dreamed of running away but, with everything secure, I was trapped, locked inside with my abusers.

The school allowed those pupils who had a home to return on certain weekends. On my first visit back, I was tempted to bolt, but I knew it was pointless because I'd be forced back and probably never be allowed home again. Instead, I decided do something else, I'd tell the toughest man I knew: my dad, he'd know what to do. But the thought of telling him that another man had touched my penis made me feel physically ill. How would I explain and what would I say? My chance came right at the end of the weekend. Dad climbed into the car, turned the key and started up the engine ready to take me back, but I hesitated and he saw.

'Is everything alright?'

It felt odd because we'd never been close and we never talked about stuff like this but I knew it was my only chance. I was genuinely terrified at the thought of going back but, try as I might, I couldn't bring myself to say that one of the staff had touched me. I was petrified Dad would think I was gay, so I told him one of the men was picking on me instead.

'Which one?' he asked, his knuckles flashing white as he gripped the steering wheel between his hands.

'The fat one,' I replied.

'And why does he pick on you?'

'I dunno, he just doesn't like me.' I shrugged. 'He just keeps picking on me all the time, it's horrible.' My body began to tremble as I spoke. 'I hate him Dad, he frightens me.'

My father looked at me and back at the road in front as he considered what to do. I could almost hear the anger bubbling up inside him. No one picked on his lad, no one. We drove the rest of the way in silence but I knew Dad had a plan.

'Right,' he said finally parking up at the back of the school. 'Show me who he is and I'll have a word.'

I followed Dad inside. By now he'd worked himself up into such a frenzy that I knew he'd tear a strip off the fat perv. Sure enough, he stormed straight into the office and everyone looked up as he walked in. Suddenly he turned to me.

'Right,' he said, 'which one is he?'

With a shaking hand, I pointed out my abuser. Not that Dad knew that part. If he had then I reckon he'd have killed the perv right there and then with his bare hands.

'You,' Dad said storming over to the fat bastard. The colour drained from his face and he turned a horrible puce colour as Dad verbally laid into him. He didn't know what had hit him as he shifted uncomfortably in his seat.

'I don't care who you are or what you represent; if you ever lay a finger on my son again I swear I'll kill you!' he bellowed.

The man looked absolutely petrified. His eyes darted nervously between me and my father as if he was trying to work out how much I'd said.

'Do you hear me?' Dad demanded getting his full attention once more. He was so angry that his head was bright purple and he was showering the fat bastard with spit.

'Yes,' the perv nodded.

I expected someone else to stick up for him but no one did. Maybe they knew what he was like.

'Right, I'm glad I've made myself clear,' my father added before storming out of the room. I ran straight after him.

'You hear that? He won't be bothering you anymore now, son.'

In that single moment I loved my father more than I'd ever done in my life. He was a tough guy, the hardest man I knew, but now he'd just become my lifesaver and hero wrapped all into one.

'There's nothing to be frightened of,' he said as he climbed back into his car and drove off.

He was right, I was never fondled again. I loved Dad for sorting it out, for stopping it overnight. The perv and his friend didn't know what or how much I'd said so they left me alone after that. At last, I felt as if I could breathe. It gave me confidence, so much so that on my next trip home I decided to run away for good. Instead of getting into the car on Sunday evening, I bolted for it. I became a fugitive and slept under hedges and in friends' sheds without their parents' knowledge. One night I even bedded down on the grass and slept next to the river, my favourite old haunt. Mates brought me food and drinks, but eventually the police came looking for me and I was captured. I started to worry.

What if the lads at school call me an attention seeker?

But I needn't have worried because, instead of being bullied, I returned a hero.

'Good lad,' one of the older boys said patting me on the back as soon as I walked back into school. As I entered the dorm, a round of applause rang out because, like a prisoner of war, I'd only done what they all wished they had.

'Quiet lads,' one of the staff members called as he walked across the room. He had one hand behind his back and ordered me to sit down on my bed.

'Right Tovey, give me your shoes,' he said holding out his hand impatiently. 'Come on lad, hurry up!' he tutted, clicking his fingers.

'But what do you want my shoes for?' I asked.

'To stop you running away again, you little sod. Now, come on, give 'em here.'

I undid my shoelaces and handed over my shoes.

'Right then,' he said producing the other hand from behind his back. 'Here you go.'

With that he threw a pair of tartan slippers onto the floor next to my feet. I looked up at him a little puzzled.

'You'll have to wear those from now on. They'll slow you up.'

I looked at the other lads and smirked. Pushing my feet into the old man-style slippers, I couldn't help but laugh because I knew they wouldn't stop me, nothing would. I expected a little banter over my snazzy footwear but no one took the piss; on the contrary, they were my runaway badge of honour.

'Well done mate,' an older lad congratulated me later that night.

'How long were you out for, a week?'

'Nah, two,' I told him.

'Good lad,' he nodded at me, his eyes full of respect.

For the first time since I arrived at this shithole, I felt good. My short burst of freedom spurred me on to plot my next escape, which came much sooner than I thought.

A staff member arranged for us to have a new space invader video game delivered to school. It was state-of-the-art and the kind you usually played down the amusement arcade. In fact, I'd spent many an hour on Minehead seafront feeding my pocket money into a similar machine, only this one was better because it was free! We crowded around as the staff member attached the lead and plugged it in. We were staggered he'd done this for us. As soon as the game fired into life his eyes widened with excitement.

'Look at that then, quality, eh?' he beamed with pride.

We all sighed appreciatively but our joy was short-lived when realised that he'd ordered the bloody thing for himself and not for us.

74

'Any chance I could get a game on that later on?' one of the older lads asked, tapping him on the shoulder. The warden's eyes didn't leave the screen, not even for a second.

'Piss off!' he hissed. 'This is too good for the likes of you.'

We looked at one another in disgust.

'What?' he asked throwing his hands up in the air one day after he'd pulled the plug. 'I don't want you lot burning it out from overuse.'

Fat chance. Instead, each day we became his audience as he slayed yet another space invader using his neon green laser cannon.

'See that lads? God, I'm good at this,' he said boring us all silly.

It was a horrible grey day outside and we'd had enough of him hogging the machine so I came up with a plan. The kids crowded around and patted him on the back as he took to the machine, just as I'd asked them to.

'Well done mate,' one said.

'Here, there's loads more coming, don't let 'em get you,' a lad called giving me a sneaky thumbs up. It was my cue to go.

My slippers were soft and cushioned against the linoleum floor so my ascent was soundless. I needn't have worried; the lads were making enough noise, cheering and calling over the sound of the game.

'Quick, they're getting faster,' another warned, pointing at the screen.

'Get your hands off,' the bloke scolded, slapping his hand away. 'Anyway,' he boasted without looking up, 'I'll soon sort them out.'

I tried not to laugh. He was on a high, cheered on by his crowd of so-called adoring fans.

His keys shone dimly in the light as they jangled from his belt. I slipped right behind him and into the general hubbub. A few of the kids had separated just enough so that I could slip my hand through. Like the artful dodger, I expertly began to unattach him from his precious bunch of metal. As if on cue, he fired a tremendous shot and the lads cheered and slapped him heavily on the back in celebration. By now they were jostling and shoving each other so much that he didn't feel the moment I slipped the keyring from the metal loop on his belt. I cupped my palm expertly around the other keys to stop them jangling, my friends parted, and I backed out and away from the crowd.

The first door was surprisingly easy to open. The place, it seemed, was deserted. The second door was also unmanned, whilst the third and main door was really no trouble at all. I could have been cruel and taken his keys with me but I knew he'd be in trouble and he would've raised the alarm much quicker. Instead, I nipped back into the common room and reattached the keys to their rightful owner. I mouthed a silent 'thank you' to my willing accomplices who were trying their best not to piss themselves laughing.

With all three doors now unlocked I simply left the building. It had taken me less than five minutes to do the impossible: escape from Colditz.

It was getting dark so no one saw me leave and head towards the road. The outside gate was locked but that wasn't a problem because, by now, I knew the fence narrowed to just three or four feet in certain places, so I simply scaled over it. I purposefully kept away from the roads because I knew the police would be out looking for me. Instead I stuck to fields and woods in a bid to stay undetected. As I followed the main country road, I heard a car approach and, convinced it was the police, I jumped into a ditch and ducked down. I carried on this way, avoiding cars but all the time keeping a look out for a passing lorry. I needed to hitch a lift – it was my only hope. Eventually, I managed to flag one down. The driver seemed a bit suspicious at first, a young lad on his own late at night but I convinced him that I lived in the next town.

'I missed my bus,' I lied.

His eyes darted down towards my tartan slippers and I tucked them carefully underneath the seat hoping he wouldn't become any more suspicious. After that I kept quiet and, to his credit, he didn't ask any more questions.

It took me two days to reach home but I made it. The first person I saw was one of my old mates from school.

'John,' he hissed, beckoning me over with his hand. He was standing behind a set of garages on the estate.

'You'd better lie low,' he warned. 'There are coppers every-where looking for you.'

'What?' I gasped.

This was going to be harder than I thought. I was pissed off because I knew it meant I couldn't go home. Instead I hid in garages and sheds, slept under bridges and under bracken in woods. I was right underneath their noses all the time but they didn't find me. In the end, starvation forced me home. To his credit, Dad seemed genuinely concerned about me.

'Where the hell have you been?' he hollered as soon as I walked in the door. I'd expected no less but this time there was something else in his eyes, something I'd never seen before. I'd expected a good hiding but didn't get one. This time I was frightened and it showed.

'I've got to call the police.' Dad sighed, picking up the phone.

I slammed my hand down and cut off the call. My father's eyes widened with anger.

'Please, please,' I begged. 'Please don't send me back there. If you do, I swear I'll kill myself.'

Within the hour the police turned up along with social services. I'd caused them quite a lot of trouble, they said. I'd brought this all on myself, they insisted. It was true, but then I had just spent a whole year locked up in a complete hellhole. Now I wanted another chance, so I begged them. I wanted to live a normal life alongside normal kids, not criminals. To my surprise, Dad fought my corner. He believed me when I said I'd top myself. It was true, I meant every word. The thought of going back there for good frightened the living daylights out of me. In the end, they decided to send me to another school. It was five miles away from home but I didn't care; anything had to be better than the last place. Just when I thought I'd been welcomed back with open arms, I realised I was mistaken. From day one I didn't have any clean clothes, a uniform or even any bus fare. I was handed a rickety old bike and told to get myself to school. Initially, I was a reformed character but it wasn't long before I started to slip back into my bad old ways.

One day, instead of cycling all the way to school I took a detour past the local DIY store I'd nicked glue from in the past. Just like before I slipped a tin of glue into my pocket and looked for somewhere I wouldn't be found. As soon as I'd inhaled the heady chemical mix, my brain buzzed and turned my body as gooey as the sticky mixture. Before long, I was glue sniffing almost every day. I hid underneath the supports of motorway bridges. They were noisy, smelly and dangerous places to be but at least I was so tucked away that no one would find me there.

Soon glue wasn't enough so I started stealing lighter fluid as well. If I couldn't get any, I'd whip the petrol caps off nearby parked cars and stick my mouth over the inlet. By sheer luck, I found an abandoned car on a piece of wasteland at the back of a council estate. It had been nicked and discarded but I was delighted when I realised it still had enough fuel inside to give off vapours. Like my secret garage stash of light ale a few years before, it became my fuel stash. The petrol fumes sent me high until I hallucinated and lost consciousness.

Occasionally, I'd put in an appearance at school just to keep social services off my back but my sniffing habit left me short-tempered and on edge. My nerves were constantly jangled. I should have been called 'Mad John' because all decent pupils avoided me like the plague. I was the boy who'd do anything for a laugh. I'd been given a second chance but I was going to blow it in spectacular style. One day, I locked myself in the storeroom because I knew that's where the teacher kept the glue to stick Perspex together. It was a particularly heady mixture and after ten minutes, I was completely off my face. I staggered out and into the corridor where I bumped into a gang of mates. They were moaning about the lockers because you had to pay £1 for a key. Now, high off my head on glue, I decided to do something about it.

'I'm gonna smash something,' I whispered to my mate. I was out of control and acting like a complete dickhead but I had no stop button and didn't know how.

'Why don't you smash up a locker?'

I laughed. It made complete sense. I wanted a locker but I couldn't afford one. It was unfair but then, so was life.

I started to kick and punch the metal with my bare fists. It hurt but I was centre of attention and I wasn't going to stop now. I kicked and pummelled at it until it was hanging off the wall. Egged on by the crowd, I yanked it clear and strode over to the window. We were high up on the first floor. I momentarily looked back at everyone and opened up a window as far as it would go. By now everyone was cheering me on and I loved it. The metal cabinet slipped immediately from my grasp and plunged quickly down towards the ground. The noise alerted a teacher on the floor below, who opened up his window to get a better look. To this day I still don't know how it missed him, but the metal locker cleared his head by a matter of millimetres. It crashed to the ground where it buckled and fell apart. I'd almost killed him: he knew it and so did I. He turned his head to look up at me; his face was as white as a sheet.

'Tovey!' he bellowed.

I backed away from the open window but it was too late, I'd been seen. The rest of the children started to chant my name so I bolted from the classroom and ran away from the school.

It took them a few hours, but the police eventually found me lying next to the abandoned car. The petrol cap was hanging off and there I was, unconscious on the floor.

CHAPTER SIX

Life on a Knife Edge

'I'M AFRAID WE can't cope with your son at this school,' the headmaster told my parents. The police had been called and the day after the locker incident we'd all been dragged in to his office, but I was the only one standing there now.

'He's not only disruptive, he causes no end of fights and usually he's the one at the centre of them all. His attendance is appalling and his attitude...' he said, peering at Dad over the top of his glasses. '...Well, his attitude leaves a lot to be desired.'

I cringed but he wasn't finished yet.

'To be frank with you, John is nothing but a thug and a hooligan who will never amount to anything in his life. I'm sorry, but as from today I'm expelling him from this school. We don't want him here – he's not only a danger to himself but to others.'

Dad shook his head in despair while Mum looked glumly

at the floor. They'd heard it all before, it wasn't any great surprise.

'As for you,' the headmaster said turning to address me. 'I'd wish you luck, but it seems the more chances you're given, the more you throw them away. If you carry on in this way then there's no hope for you.'

Of course, I got a good hiding when I got home but it didn't change a thing. The next day, with Mum in bed and Dad back at work, I sniffed glue just to pass the time. With nothing better to do, I hung around the school gates – my old and original school – hoping to catch a glimpse of my mates. But as soon as the teachers saw me, they shooed me away; they knew what I was like, the little sod who had brought them nothing but trouble. What did I expect?

Fuck 'em, I thought. *Fuck 'em all. They said I'd never amount to much so I'll prove them right.*

I took to the streets like a wolf seeking out prey. I stalked around the neighbourhood, hanging around in the shadows looking, watching and waiting for an opportunity to steal.

One afternoon I nipped around the back of some local shops. It was a warm day and the door was slightly ajar to let the cool air flow through and that's when I saw it, through the crack in the door. A purse on the worktop, right next to the kettle. Sneaking in, I prised it open and took out a wad of notes. I gasped – there was £80 to £100 inside, I'd just hit the jackpot! But I wasn't greedy, I didn't need it all. I peeled off two £10 notes and tucked them neatly into my back pocket before putting the rest back in the purse. I placed it down exactly where I'd found it and tiptoed back out through the door before sprinting off down the alleyway. It was that easy. I spent the money on lighter fuel and glue.

I broke into garages or sheds just to see what I could steal. Thankfully, there weren't many drugs around when I was younger, only hash, and I'm glad because by now, I was acting like a class A junkie looking for his next fix.

One afternoon I was bored and off my face on cider when I decided to take revenge on a lad in my neighbourhood who'd given me a shove. I grabbed a rounders bat, strolled over to his house and shouted out his name in the middle of the street. When he didn't appear, I smashed every window in his house. The noise of breaking glass alerted neighbours who frantically called the police. I was arrested and charged with criminal damage. When my father found out he went mad. He was thoroughly ashamed of me, as was the rest of my family. Stupidly, I believed that going to court would make me a tough guy and someone to be respected. I was an idiot. I was given a conditional discharge but now, at just 16, I had a criminal record, something that would follow and haunt me throughout the rest of my life. Of course, I received another good hiding when I went home but I didn't care. I was beyond help.

It was decided that to keep me on the right track I should be sent to a youth centre for troubled teenagers but there was one problem: it was two bus rides away. For once, I was given enough money for the bus fare, anything to keep me on the straight and narrow. However, it also meant early starts, and I had to leave the house at 7am to make it there for 9am. Getting home was an equal nightmare. The centre was okay because at least we were allowed to smoke there. To me it was just a waiting room until I was legally allowed to sign on. Sometimes, I'd get to the end of the road before deciding that I really couldn't be arsed to go in, and I'd turn back.

Other times I'd bunk off in the middle of the city centre, stopping off at shops to steal my dinner. In many ways I was still a child but old enough to realise I'd been thrown on the scrap heap of life, and I deserved it.

But there was something else making me feel despondent and that was my health. I'd suddenly started to feel ill and totally washed out. The two hour bus journey seemed to take forever and all I wanted to do was sleep. When I woke up in the morning I felt as if I hadn't even been to bed. Just dragging myself up, getting dressed and eating breakfast felt like I was climbing a mountain. I was thirsty too, all the time. I'd drink and drink but nothing seemed to quench my thirst.

'John's taken all the milk,' my brother complained one morning.

I ran out of the house before I got a good hiding. I didn't understand and certainly couldn't help it. No matter how much I drank, I always seemed to need and want more.

One morning I was knackered and by the time I'd reached the end of our street, I was so exhausted that I bunked off, not to glue sniff but to sleep. I slept all day. It was only as dusk approached and cold set in that I actually woke up and wandered back home. My parents didn't know where I'd been and I didn't elaborate. But the first thing I did as soon as I got in was drink a pint of water and go straight to bed. Something wasn't right, but I was only 16 and I didn't have a clue what was wrong. In the meantime, my mood swings and aggression continued to escalate. Eventually my non-attendance caught up with me and Dad received a phone call from a member of staff at the centre.

'Why you little sod!' he shouted, slamming down the phone.

After that, my parents watched my every move and became even stricter.

'Stop turning the bloody tap on!' Mum snapped, slamming the kettle down on top of the work surface.

But I was so thirsty that I permanently had my mouth open underneath the kitchen tap like a fish.

'Tony, he's at it again,' she called to Dad.

'Get away from there,' he stormed. 'What the hell's the matter with you?'

But I didn't know. I didn't understand why my mouth was always as dry as the Sahara desert. Moments later I was upstairs in the bathroom doing exactly the same thing.

'I told you,' Dad warned me from the other side of the door.

I turned off the cold tap. After that, we played a game of cat and mouse. I'd turn on the bathroom tap and try to disguise it with a flush of the toilet but Dad always heard.

'Turn that bloody tap off!'

In the end, I was so desperate that I'd flush the toilet just so I could cup my hands inside it to catch a few precious drops of water. It was disgusting but I couldn't satisfy my thirst. My clothes started to get loose and my once tight jeans hung now from my skeletal frame. I was losing weight fast. I was almost six foot tall but when I stepped on Mum's scales, I weighed a shocking six stone and looked like a walking skeleton.

One day, I was at the centre doing some woodwork when a vicious thirst overwhelmed me. I dipped my head underneath the tap and began to drink greedily. The teacher was so angry that he threw a block of wood at the back of my head.

'Tovey, get away from there. Do some work and stop drinking water!'

'But I'm thirsty,' I pleaded.

'It'll be all those nights walking the street boozing and glue sniffing, they're catching you up son. You need to look after yourself,' he added sarcastically.

Maybe he had a point? Maybe I'd knackered my body with all the solvent abuse?

A few days later, I was in the bedroom getting dressed when Anthony walked in. As soon as he saw me, he stopped dead in his tracks.

'John, you look like a skeleton!'

I glanced down at my protruding hip bones and ribs. I looked and felt disgusting. By now I was so weak that I just about managed the stairs down to the front room. Once there, I collapsed into a heap on the sofa. The rest of the afternoon was a bit hazy but I was later told that I drifted in and out of consciousness.

My parents called a doctor who diagnosed dehydration.

'You just need to drink something,' he said packing up his bag as he left the house.

My parents took him at his word. This was nothing but a bout of attention-seeking. I just needed fluids, that's all. But Clair suspected otherwise and called an ambulance. By the time it arrived I was too weak to even stand.

'Let me carry him,' she offered.

My lovely sister scooped me up in her arms and took me outside and into the waiting ambulance. By the time we reached the hospital I was put on a drip.

'He's got diabetes,' a doctor informed my family. 'It's a good job you got him here when you did – another couple of hours and he would have died.'

But I was far too ill to take any notice. All I remember is a sense of relief because I was still alive. I stayed in hospital for three weeks and loved it because, not only did I get three square meals a day, but the place was warm. I was used to a freezing cold, dirty house so this was luxury in comparison. I didn't want to go home or return to my old life.

There was a TV room but I was too weak to walk down the corridor so instead I got out my old tape player and listened to the new Madness album, ironically called *Keep Moving*. It kept me going during those long three weeks. I'd sing along to the Michael Caine track, and make the nurses laugh by mimicking his voice. If nothing else, I still knew how to charm the ladies.

Initially, I returned home physically and mentally stronger. For the first time I even felt positive about the future. The diabetes meant I had to inject myself with insulin twice a day to stop me from getting sick but at least I felt human again.

One day Mum was watching from a corner of the room as I pushed the needle into my skin. She couldn't help herself.

'You deserve that for all you've put us through, you deserve diabetes. You've done it to yourself and now you'll have to do that for the rest of your life,' she hissed pointing at the needle. 'It serves you right.'

My mouth hung open in horror at my own mother's words. I realised then just how cruel she was. A five foot three mound of misery, dressed in jumble sale clothes and a dirty old headscarf. I'd hoped that once I'd returned home she'd stop thinking about herself and finally start acting like a proper mum but I was wrong. If the shock of my illness wouldn't change her, nothing would.

My diabetes meant I had to eat often. At first there was an abundance of healthy foods bought by Mum, including brown bread, which was more expensive than the regular white stuff. But after a while, the healthy food petered out because she gave up buying it and we returned to tinned dinners. Nothing had changed. Sometimes the cupboard would be bare and I'd be scratching around looking for something, anything to eat.

I was right at the end of my education but Dad insisted I return to the centre to finish off the course. I didn't see much point. I wasn't going to leave with any qualifications and besides, there were only a few more weeks left to go. But he wouldn't back down so off I went, two hours and two buses in the morning and the same again at night. Three evenings a week we'd have to stay behind for extra lessons so I wouldn't get home until gone 10pm – I was permanently knackered.

The hospital had mended me physically but I soon realised I was far from being fixed mentally. The whole nature of my diabetes mixed with hormonal changes, meant I was continually on edge. I was so emotional, I thought I'd burst into tears at any moment and I longed to feel normal again.

One night, I stayed late but caught the next bus back into Bristol. I was just walking to the second bus stop when I heard my name being called. I turned around to see two lads from the approved school unit standing there. I felt my body stiffen because these weren't nice blokes; they were from the old locked unit, the one I'd been glad to leave behind. Only they were a few years older than me so they'd already left.

'Where you going?' one asked.

'Back home. I'm just on my way to the bus.' I said pointing over towards the bus stop. I felt nervous just seeing them again because I found them so intimidating.

'Aww, don't be wet,' he said coaxing me away. 'Come with us, we're off to have some fun.'

I thought about the bus and how I really ought to be getting home. I wanted to refuse but I knew what these lads were like, and I was scared because I knew they wouldn't take no for an answer.

'Don't be so fucking boring mate,' the other lad teased. 'Come with us. What's the matter? You a good boy now all of a sudden?'

I shrugged my shoulders and tried to relax. What harm could it do? Besides, I'd just catch a later bus.

'Fuck it, go on then!' I laughed with bravado.

'Champion!' he said patting me on the back. 'Good man. Now we've got a little something here if you want to have a drink?'

He opened up his jacket to reveal a full bottle of sherry.

'Go on, take a sip.'

I did as he said and passed the bottle back to him.

'Nah, we've got some more of that stuff. Take it. It's yours.'

I grinned and screwed the lid back on.

'Thanks,' I replied. 'Right,' I said longing to be part of a gang again, 'where are we off to?'

'Car park,' the older lad directed. 'It's more private there.'

I looked at him, a bit baffled.

'We've got some glue,' he whispered as he opened up the top of a carrier bag.

He tapped the side of his nose with a finger and scrunched the bag back up in his hand.

'Come on you dickhead, let's get going.'

The three of us walked to the nearest multi-storey car park where we climbed up flights of stairs to one of the more deserted levels. I drank the sherry and sniffed the glue. My head began to buzz and feel light but instead of stopping, I sniffed some more. Eventually, everything went black.

I woke to the sound of an unfamiliar voice.

'Come on son, wake up.'

I opened my eyes but everything was blurred. I tried to focus and when I did, I realised that the lads had scarpered. The voice belonged to a police officer. I felt disorientated and looked around to get my bearings. I was still in the car park but lying on the concrete floor. My legs were freezing. I glanced down, the sherry bottle was at my side, and so was the plastic bag. But my trousers and pants had been pulled down to my ankles. I hitched myself up and tried to grab at them to pull them back up but my head was throbbing and I felt woozy and sick. As the police officers lifted me to my feet, I managed to dip down and pull my trousers up. I felt utterly ashamed. Just then something dripped against my face, and I put my fingers up to catch it –it was blood coming from my nose. It was bleeding heavy as though I'd been punched straight in the face. My hand drifted towards my eye, which also felt sticky. It was swollen and sore beneath my touch and the surrounding skin had split open. I felt a pain in my hand. It was covered in blood but not from the cuts, something or someone had split that open too. My fingers were squashed as if they'd been stamped on. I looked around and realised my jacket was missing.

'My coat,' I muttered.

'Hey steady son, you've got a right shiner there,' the officer said gripping my arm.

I thought they were there to help me but instead of going to hospital, I was arrested, locked in a cell and charged with vagrancy. I told the police I was diabetic and needed my insulin but they didn't call a doctor; instead they threw me a chocolate bar. I begged them not to tell my parents but because of my age, they had to take me home.

'Can't you just drop me on the corner or something? I promise I'll go straight home,' I pleaded as we travelled in the squad car.

The officer shook his head.

'Sorry son, we're responsible for you until you're back in the arms of your loving parents.' He grinned as his mate laughed.

My heart sank. Of course, my parents went ballistic.

'That's why I can't go out anymore,' Mum wailed. 'You've made me a virtual recluse. I'm too ashamed to go out because everyone knows who I am. Everyone knows I'm your mother. All you do is bring the police to our door, why can't you be normal?'

I was given another good hiding but I was still so anesthetised by the drink and glue that I didn't feel any pain until the following morning. My life was on a downward spiral and not for the first time. Sometimes I dreamed of dying in my bed. Surely it'd be best all round if I just faded away?

A few days later I appeared at the Youth Court where I was fined £20.

'I hope you're proud of yourself,' Dad muttered as we left court. I hung my head in shame. I knew I needed to sort myself out but just couldn't seem to do it.

Not long afterwards, I finished school and went to sign on. A fortnight later, I was at the Jobcentre when I spotted an ad for a double-glazing salesman. I applied for the job and, to my amazement, I got it. I thought my parents would be pleased but they didn't seem that impressed.

'I need a new suit,' I announced later that day.

'Why?' Mum asked, eying me suspiciously.

'Because I got myself a job,' I said proudly puffing out my chest.

'A job?' she said sitting up and stubbing out the remainder of her fag in the ashtray. 'Doing what?'

'I'm going to sell double-glazing.' I beamed proudly as though I'd just landed the best career opportunity in the world.

Mum laughed.

'You can wear those black trousers you've got, and I'll find you a pair of shoes.'

I shuddered; she meant more jumble sale shoes. Needless to say, when a scruffy oik like me turned up on people's doorsteps no one bought a thing.

'You need to smarten up your act if you want to make a sale,' my boss ordered, looking me up and down with disgust. My shoes were too small, my trousers threadbare and my shirt old and creased.

'When do I get paid?' I asked hopefully.

'When you make a sale,' he said slamming his fist down on the desk.

I never did make a sale so I never got paid and my career was over in two short weeks.

'Ha, I knew you wouldn't last,' Mum crowed when I told her.

The Jobcentre tried again, this time sending me on a youth training scheme with one of my old mates from school called Simon. It was called a construction job but really it was just slave labour. We did a week's induction before being let loose on a building site and although it was strict the other lads were school drop outs too, so I fitted in well. On my first week in the job, I was sent with a lad called Lee to clear out a ditch. It was Lee's first week too and, because he'd arrived on site on his motorbike, he was given the keys to a dumper truck and told to drive it. The dumper truck was seven-and-a-half tonnes of pure machinery. It needed to be treated with respect and with proper training and handling, but being kids we just did as we were told. I was standing in the ditch clearing it out with my bare hands when Lee jumped into the driver's seat. It fired into life as black diesel smoke chugged out of the exhaust. Lee had never driven anything like it before in his life and was just doing what he'd been told. Suddenly, the machine turned back towards the ditch. It seemed to slip and then there was an almighty creak as it tipped over towards me.

This is it, I thought. *This is the moment I'm going to die.*

I fell backwards and closed my eyes. I'd spent so long thinking of my death and now finally, here it was. An excruciating pain shot through my body but as I opened my eyes, I realised that as I'd fallen, I'd sunk into the soft damp earth beneath me – it had saved my life. But with the machine wedged against my lap I was trapped. One of the wheels pressed against my body from the waist down and I was in agony. I couldn't see clearly. I guessed that Lee had fallen awkwardly and somehow trapped his foot against the accelerator. I called again but it was impossible to hear above the deafening noise. I wondered why he hadn't come to help me? There was no one else there, only the two of us. I shouted again but I could barely hear my own voice over the din of the revving engine.

'Help!' I screamed in agony.

Black diesel fumes filled the ditch and started choking my lungs. I screamed and screamed but my exhausted voice gave way to nothing. Still the engine revved. Plumes of smoke rose high up into the air, and I prayed that someone would spot them and bring help soon. I didn't know it at the time, but a dog walker on the opposite side of the River Avon had heard the deafening noise and seen the smoke. He alerted some lads at the other site who dashed over. Eventually, I felt a hand on my shoulder and I sighed with relief. I'd never been so grateful to see anyone more in my life.

'John, John, are you okay?' my colleague asked.

I nodded numbly although I was far from it.

'John, listen, where's Lee?'

'I don't know,' I replied truthfully. 'He was driving the dumper but he missed the turn. The next thing I knew it came hurtling over towards me. Jesus, it's my leg, it's killing me. Please help me. Please get this thing off me.' I was hysterical.

My colleague looked ashen-faced then he turned to ask me something.

'John, was Lee wearing a denim jacket?'

It was a ridiculous question and I wasn't sure why he was asking but I winced and nodded. He looked as if he was going to be sick but I followed his eye line. It was hard to make out from where I was lying, but I could just see the faint outline of an arm coming up from the ground underneath the truck. It was clad in denim.

Almost an hour after the accident a JCB was brought in to help move the digger. Someone called an ambulance and I was rushed to Bristol Royal Infirmary, where I was told I'd broken both my leg and hip. The main nerve in my leg had also been crushed and was severely damaged but at least I was alive. Lee hadn't been so lucky. It was the nurses who finally told me. I asked and asked until one of them did the decent thing and broke the devastating news that Lee had been killed. He was just 16 years old. As I recovered in hospital, I felt plagued with guilt. It should have been me, not Lee. He was a lovely lad and a good person who came from a loving family.

A few days later I spotted an old picture of him on the front page of the local paper. He was smiling with his family somewhere sunny on holiday; I thought my heart would break. Lee didn't deserve to die.

I was a total and utter piece of shit and, if anyone deserved to lose their life that day, it was me.

CHAPTER SEVEN

Out of Control

'HERE HE IS,' a voice called from behind the hospital curtain.

'Hey!' I said a smile beaming across my face. It was the first time I'd smiled since the accident.

I looked up to see Simon, my work mate. I was delighted to see him.

'What have you been up to then?' another voice chirped as a second face peeped around the curtain. It was Dexter, another good mate from work. He'd come too.

It was great to see them both. Since the accident, I'd done nothing but think about Lee, and what might have been. If only I'd been given the keys to the digger and not him. If only I'd driven it. He deserved to live, I didn't. Lee was a good person but I wasn't and I felt guilty just for breathing.

'Here,' Simon said, opening up the carrier bag in his hands. He plonked himself down onto the chair at the side of my bed. I was pretty immobile with my leg in plaster but curiosity got the better of me and I craned my neck to see what he'd brought. Grapes, perhaps? Nah, too obvious and these were blokes, after all. Maybe it was a paper to read?

'What is it?' I asked, straining my neck.

'The best aid to recovery in the world,' Simon announced. 'Your Madness tapes!'

The second smile of the day broke across my face but then my heart sank.

'I haven't got anything to play them on,' I sighed.

'Ah,' he said gesturing over to Dexter. 'That's why we brought you this.'

'Ta-dah!' said Dexter, laughing as he pulled out my old battered tape recorder from behind his back.

The tape machine door was broken and you had to cram the tape in at the front but it worked fine. I didn't care what it looked like as long as it played my music. I was a tough lad but I could've kissed them both. They were right, Madness was my favourite band and I knew with their albums playing loud and clear in my ear, I'd soon be up and about again. But my injuries were pretty bad: as well as multiple broken bones, the main nerve in my leg was so badly damaged that I was weak down my left hand side. In fact, my side was so weak that I whenever I tried to put any weight on my leg it would wobble and tremor beneath me like a plate of jelly. The longer it took to heal, the more convinced I became that I'd be paralysed for the rest of my life, but the nurses had other ideas.

'Come on John, up you get,' one said bright and early the following morning. She pulled back the sheet and blanket on my bed and I felt the cold ward air against my skin.

'What time is it?' I asked, bleary-eyed.

'It's 7.30am, but you need to have your breakfast and get sorted out.'

'Why?' I yawned stretching my arms above my head.

'Today you're going for electrotherapy to help stimulate your weakened leg muscle.'

My left leg and hip had been reset and covered in plaster. However, because I'd spent so long in my hospital bed my leg had begun to waste away, but now it was time to get it moving again.

When the nurses came to collect me for treatment later that morning, I was waiting. As they approached I quickly pressed down the play button on the tape recorder. 'One Step Beyond' echoed loudly across the ward and we began to laugh. I loved the nurses on the ward, they were a real tonic. They even helped me inject myself with insulin when I found it difficult to move. Slowly, I started to regain my strength and, although I knew my leg would never be the same again, my age helped it heal much quicker than the doctors had first predicted. I also think my music played a small part too – the power of Madness! Before long, it was time to return home, albeit balanced on a pair of shiny steel crutches.

'Mind how you go,' my favourite nurse said giving me a pat on the back as I hobbled past.

'Thanks,' I grinned. 'Thanks for everything!' I shouted without turning back. I had just got into my stride when I heard the nurse's voice calling to me along the corridor.

'And John,' she said.

I stopped in my tracks and manoeuvred the crutches so that I could turn back to face her.

'Mind how you go,' she smiled.

'Will do,' I grinned cheekily and then I was on my way.

I was in two minds leaving hospital that day. Part of me felt desperate to leave the confines of the ward and live life again, whilst the other part loved and craved the feeling of being looked after. I hopped into the ambulance and went home. I'd hoped that Dad might come and collect me but he was busy at work.

The doctors later removed my cast and fitted my leg with a splint. It felt odd and restrictive; the board was rough and it rubbed against the side of my knee, but at least I was back on my feet again.

Back at home, and try as I might, I just couldn't shake the vision of Lee out of my head. I listened to my music to try and erase it from my memory but there it was, always in the background. It haunted my every waking hour. Even when I was asleep, the horror vision would seep in and take over my nightmares. It replayed time and time again like a sick film trailer inside my head but I wasn't ever able to save him no matter how hard I tried. A deep depression swept over me and choked me in darkness. Like Mum, I became a virtual recluse. I locked myself in my room and took solace in my music. My head constantly spun with black thoughts, like a washing machine with house bricks inside. I'd had no counselling and it showed. No one ever asked me about the accident, instead it was all hushed up.

One day, a reporter from the local paper called at the door to speak to me but Dad sent him packing. Even my father knew I was emotionally brittle. My physical injuries were healing slowly but the mental scars ran deep and wide.

My seventeenth birthday came and went but I didn't feel much like celebrating and I was acting as if my life was already over. I knew that in order to get better I had to get myself back out of the house again. I practised each day until I became a dab hand on my crutches. In fact, I was so good that if there'd been a 100 metres crutches race, I'd have won hands down!

'Where you going?' Mum asked one evening as I limped towards the door.

'Youth club,' I replied, shutting it behind me.

I rested my crutches on the path and off I went, like greased lightning. The metal poles took each step in place of my withered left leg. *Tap, tap, tap,* they went as I made my way along the street. Finally after a good ten-minute hop, I saw the lights of the youth club glowing in the distance. It was hot inside with not enough air and too many kids running around. I watched them cautiously; I didn't want anyone tripping over my crutches because it would have taken me clean to the floor. A few people wandered over to ask how I was.

'I'm fine,' I told them but I wasn't, not really.

The 'Nelly the Elephant' song by the Toy Dolls blasted loud over the speaker and everyone cheered and began to dance. Even though I was propped up on crutches, it didn't stop me. I started dancing, trying to keep up with the others. This was a punk version and, despite my broken leg, I was determined to enjoy myself. Soon I'd lost control and started lashing out at everyone and everything with my crutches – the dance equivalent of a metal sprinkler – showering everyone with a slap on the way. Within minutes the dance floor had cleared and I was all alone, John Tovey, the local nutty boy having a mental fit. I heard a loud scratch as someone whipped the needle off the record halfway through and stopped the song. That's when I realised everyone's eyes were on me. I should have felt embarrassed, but I didn't care, I stood there defiantly waiting for someone, anyone to say something. No one did. I glanced across the room and that's when I spotted the back of his head, a lad who owed me money from ages ago. He'd been avoiding me but now I was here and it was payback time.

'You owe me,' I said, my voice deep and menacing as I stood directly behind him.

I watched his body shrink as he recognised my voice. He gulped and slowly turned to face me. All the colour had drained from his face as if he'd seen a ghost.

'I... I heard you'd been in an accident...' he stammered.

'Yeah, but I'm here now, and I want my money back,' I demanded holding out my hand.

The kid's eyes darted around the room as if looking for an escape.

'I'll give it to you soon,' he insisted. 'It's just I don't have anything on me right now.'

A red mist descended. I knew it was bullshit so I head-butted him to the ground. A group of kids gathered around to watch. I looked up but no one dared catch my eye, they all knew better. I might have looked weak, pathetic and broken on my metal crutches but underneath I was still the same old John Tovey, local nutter and yob. After that, I just went crazy. Someone tried to drag me off and the kid ran out. A youth worker grabbed me and took me through to the office to try and calm me down because I was shaking with anger. Moments later, the door flew open and in walked the boy's father, followed close behind by his mother, who started shouting and calling me all the names under the sun.

'Is this him?' the dad asked, pointing directly at me.

His son nodded.

'Right, I want a word with you.'

It was all I needed and I went crazy a second time. My arms sprayed all around lashing out and I beat the dad up too. At one point I even managed to drag open the curtains so that all my friends could see what was happening outside. I was out of control and I battered the poor man black and blue. Someone called the police who arrived minutes later with sirens blaring. I was arrested and dragged out of the centre with my leg in a splint, and my arms held high up my back.

'Don't tell my dad,' I begged as they led me to the squad car.

'You should have thought of that earlier,' a copper replied.

Despite my crutches, I was locked up in a police cell overnight before being charged and released the following morning. Thankfully, because I was 17, I was old enough to attend court alone which I did, three weeks later. I pleaded guilty to two counts of ABH and was given two years probation, community service and a huge £300 fine. I didn't tell a soul but it didn't matter because my escapade had made the front page of the local paper and it wasn't long before the whole estate knew, including my parents. Of course, they went crackers.

After that, I was in and out of trouble all the time. My leg had healed but it just gave me more scope to go out and shoplift because I was quicker without my crutches. I had no job, no prospects and I was fast becoming a hostile character and an anti-social yob who filled his days with cider. I shaved all my hair off a second time and started knocking around with local skinheads – it felt good to be part of a gang again. Not surprisingly, we ended up in fights with rival gangs and I was up in front of the judge again and again.

My parents had reached breaking point. One day Mum marched upstairs to fetch something. As I heard her rooting around in my bedroom I sat bolt upright on the sofa. The living room door swung open and I saw her standing there in the doorway with a pile of something in her hands, which she threw down. They landed on the filthy floor with a clatter and scattered all around. I gasped when I realised what they were – my beloved Madness albums.

'Let's destroy something you love so you can see how it feels,' Mum hissed before pressing the heel of her shoe down on each and every record. The cracking noise sickened me as they shattered and splintered beneath her feet.

'No!' I begged but my distress fired her up even more.

I hated my mother more in that moment than I'd ever done before in my life. I knew I had to escape before I did something stupid so I fled the house and vowed never to return. I meant it. There was nothing worth going back for.

Inevitably, along with my new law-breaking mates I got into even more trouble, this time a fight at a bus station in Taunton. When the police finally handcuffed me, I didn't bother to deny it. But, when the custody sergeant rang to ask my parents if they could bring me home, Mum refused. With no address to go to, I was remanded for three weeks inside Exeter prison's youth custody section. It was meant to be a short, sharp shock but it didn't work. I'd been in a similar place before so I knew what to expect. The only difference was that back then I'd been a child but now I was older and so more able to take care of myself. It became my natural home.

I was brought before the court where I admitted ABH and ordered to go to an attendance centre as part of my punishment, a total of 24 hours over 12 weeks. It was called punishment but I loved it! A sergeant major type was put in charge and he forced us to do press-ups and gruelling circuits around the yard. It was meant to keep us focused and out of trouble but, unlike the others, I enjoyed it. I wanted to be pushed to the edge just to see how far I could go. As part of our rehabilitation we made toys for the local children's hospital. I sewed the eyes on dollies and teddies – completely at odds with my aggressive appearance. I had a shaved head, cheap tattoos, an extensive criminal record and I was still only 17 years old. I was a lost cause, a burden on society and an embarrassment to my family and all who knew me. However, even though I didn't really deserve it, someone was about to throw me a valuable lifeline. I was about to get my first proper job.

CHAPTER EIGHT

New Start

DESPITE MY BEST attempts to wreck my life before it had even started, someone somewhere saw something in me that I couldn't even see in myself and he offered me a job at a local firm. I was thrilled because it was my first stroke of good luck, a chance to prove myself and I was determined not to mess it up. I'd been sleeping rough on friends' floors and generally overstaying my welcome so I was grateful for the chance to get back on my feet again.

It wasn't a particularly glamorous position, working as a store man for a pest control company, but it was mine. I had two bosses and one in particular was a really friendly fella, his name was Brian. I'd been referred to Brian through the youth employment scheme. I knew the pay wasn't great but the job had its bonuses, namely being in the village where I lived so I was determined to get it. Of course, when Brian asked me about my schooling, I lied and sugar-coated my chequered past. I told him I'd been at the same secondary school for the past five years and thankfully, he believed me. Although I was constantly worried that he'd find out, I thought it was a risk worth taking. Brian put his trust in me and in the bargain promised to pay me £40 a week, more money than I'd ever had in my life.

'I'll work hard for you,' I insisted when he broke the good news.

'I hope so John,' he replied. 'Just don't let me down.'

My job involved checking and moving stock around the storeroom and steam-cleaning the filters that were used to rid the air of cigarette smoke. I loved my job because I was left to my own devices in a storeroom, which became my own private 'office'. It was a long, thin room and pretty basic with no heating or natural light, and was packed from floor to ceiling with cleaning products and boxes. But I didn't care, to me that cramped room represented my own little kingdom where I was in charge with no one to nag or tell me what to do.

My parents were so impressed that they even let me have my old bedroom back, which made life even easier. I loved my job working for Brian. He left me alone and, most days, I'd just close the door on the rest of the world and beaver away getting the job done, listening to Madness. Even on the long and boring days, my Madness songs helped me through. At that time the group had just released a new album, *Mad Not Mad*. Lots of people had panned it but I lapped it up and played it over and over again on my battered old tape recorder which I'd taken into work.

With a bit of cash in my pocket, I was able to start living

my life. I splashed out on some nice trendy clothes and threw away all my old jumble sale hand-me-downs. For the first time in my life I felt as if I belonged, not only in the world but in society.

In autumn 1985 I heard the best news ever: Madness were coming to do a gig in Bristol. It was as if all my birthdays had come at once. Eager to see my idols I queued from the crack of dawn long before the box office had even opened. When it did, I bought two tickets, one for me and one for Anthony. The tickets were cheap – only £5.50 – and it was a small price to pay to watch my heroes perform in the flesh. The lads in Madness felt like older brothers to me; their songs and lyrics had helped me through some of the darkest times of my life and made me realise that no matter how bleak things were, there was always light at the end of the tunnel.

There was a rumour circulating that the band was going to do a sound check at Colston Hall in Bristol, where they were due to perform later that night. It was a freezing cold November day, but I knew that if the rumour was right, it was too good an opportunity to miss. Anthony and I arrived bright and early, around 9am. But as the day passed by Anthony wandered off into town to kill some time whilst I stood there getting colder and colder. I was hungry and thirsty but there was no way I was moving from the stage door. I'd have waited all week if I'd had to. More and more fans arrived but still I refused to budge or be jostled from my prime position. It was just starting to get dark when someone spotted a car pulling up. It stopped right behind the crowd and a silence descended amongst the fans as my heroes stepped onto the pavement – Suggs and Lee Thompson. I couldn't believe it because out of the whole band they were my favourite members and Anthony had missed them. My fingers were as frozen as blocks of ice, but I pushed my way forward through the throng. Despite the bitter cold and other fans vying for best position somehow I managed to break through to the front of the group. The crowd retreated backwards as Suggs made his way through towards the stage door. I remained where I was when suddenly, I found myself standing right in front of the man himself. I was absolutely dumbstruck as he acknowledged me with a grin. I was quite literally frozen to the spot. Unlike me, Suggs had dressed for the weather in a sensible sheepskin coat. I think the shock of actually seeing him combined with the arctic cold affected my brain because within seconds I was gibbering away like an idiot.

'Hello, Suggs,' I whimpered like a girl, 'the new album is brilliant.'

'Ah thank you my fine man,' Suggs replied graciously with a smile. He lifted his hand and took a drag from a roll up cigarette that he was holding between his fingers. I watched as the embers glowed brightly.

When he drops it, I'll take it as a souvenir, I thought making a mental note to myself.

I was watching the cigarette like a hawk when I spotted another figure approach from behind – it was Lee Thompson, a man who in my opinion is the finest lyricist in the country. I pushed past Suggs and ran towards Lee.

'You write the best songs ever!' I gushed. I meant every word.

Lee's songs were so spot on that I felt as though he'd written them about me and my crappy life. I'd read somewhere that Lee had had a similar upbringing so I knew he understood what it felt like to be me.

'Thanks very much,' he replied shaking my hand. I vowed never to wash it again.

I thought Suggs had been well dressed, but Lee looked even cooler in his smart black jacket and cap.

By now I was getting jostled by other fans all wanting to get close so I knew I didn't have long. I asked them if they'd sign my nutty boys T-shirt and was thrilled when they agreed, signing their names by their respective faces. Then I handed Suggs an American flag – a promotional item I'd got free with their Uncle Sam single – it had Russian writing on it but Suggs signed that too. Moments later, someone opened the backstage door and in an instant my heroes had gone. But I'd done what I'd come here to do: I'd met the main members of the band. Starving hungry, but satisfied my day's experience couldn't be topped, I wandered off in search of food. You can imagine how pissed off I was when I later found out the rest of the band had arrived just minutes after I'd left!

Anthony came to find me but was gutted when I told him what he'd missed. Then we walked to a nearby burger bar so that we could both defrost. Afterwards, we called at an off-licence so I could buy a tin of cider before heading back to the venue, ready for the gig at 7pm. As I walked along the street I was still floating on air, not through booze, but just because I'd met them.

When we arrived, the hall was hot and packed with nutty boys and girls all there to see the greatest band in the world. The atmosphere was electric, with everyone watching and waiting for Madness to appear. As soon as the lights dimmed and Chas's voice boomed over the mic, the room went crazy. It was bedlam mixed with utter joy. We were supposed to sit in our seats but as soon as I saw the boys I jumped to my feet. Others followed but I was quick off the mark and made it to the front first. I guarded my space placing my elbows flat on the floor of the stage to secure my spot throughout the show. Madness sang their way through one hit to another and the crowd bounced up and down appreciatively in time to the music. The beat was so infectious that, if I could have been frozen in that moment I would because I knew life didn't get much better than this. Despite a rowdy crowd, I managed to stay at the front. I looked back to see if I could spot Anthony; I couldn't but I knew he was old enough to look after himself. I looked up at the stage to see band member Chris Foreman standing right in front of me, wearing bright red Doc Martens. They were so cool that I wanted to reach out and touch them. The crowd swayed behind knocking me sideways but I just about managed to stretch out my hand far enough to tap one of his boots. It sounds mad but that's how crackers I was about them.

At the end of the gig I ran outside along with other die-hard fans back to the stage door. Moments later our heroes appeared. They graciously thanked the crowd but for me it wasn't enough. I pushed my way through to the front and managed to inch in right next to Suggs.

'Do you mind if we have a picture Mr Suggs?' I asked. I was nervous and the words came tumbling out of my mouth before I'd had chance to think what I was saying.

Mr Suggs? I cringed inside. *Had I really just said that?*

But Suggs was a complete gentleman and politely obliged, even shaking my hand into the bargain. A friend of mine who also happened to be outside stage door after the gig held up a camera and pressed the shutter.

'Thanks!' I said trying to regain my composure.

'No problem.' Suggs smiled before making his way to the waiting coach.

My mate ran up and grabbed me by the arm.

'That's gonna be a fucking brilliant picture!' he squealed, unable to contain his excitement. 'Suggs was looking right at you when he shook your hand. You looked like best mates!'

'Really? I hope it turns out!'

But my eyes were busy searching for the rest of the band who'd already climbed onto the waiting coach. My heart sank, I was determined I wasn't going to miss them twice in one day. As the other fans stood there wondering what to do I saw my chance. The band had opened a top window and the group were waving through it. I glanced down; the window was towards the back of the bus just above the wheel. Without warning, I broke free and, with a running jump, hopped up onto the back wheel. A pain shot through my leg, which was still healing. I winced but my agony was soon forgotten when the lads started to shake my hand. Now I really had met them all.

'Get down off there you nutter!' Chas called down to me through the open window.

I looked up at him and grinned like an idiot.

'You'll break your bloody neck!'

The rest of the band urged me to jump down. I don't think they wanted a squashed fan on their hands.

'I don't care,' I shouted and the truth was I didn't. This was the best moment of my shitty little life and I didn't want it to end.

'I love your band,' I called like a deranged stalker. 'I love you guys, you've saved my life!'

They nodded gratefully but were more concerned about me slipping under the wheel of their bus. Reluctantly, I climbed down and waved with the others from the path. Deep down I knew, and so did Madness, that if I could I would have climbed in there with them. I'd have risked it all because that band had saved my life.

When I returned to work the following Monday, I was on a high and played my tapes louder than ever. If anything, I was even nuttier about the nutty boys. Finally, my life was on the up. I'd even managed to knock solvent abuse on the head, but in reality all I did was replace one addiction with another and I replaced glue with football.

I'd always been a massive Bristol City fan and my love for them was undying. Outside work, I'd go to every match both home and away. For a whole year I kept out of trouble. It was the best year of my life but then I got involved with a different kind of trouble: football violence. I was a freelance fighter. No gangs, just me on my own against the world. Other fans would cheer me on and, if anything erupted, I'd be the first to wade in; I didn't hit just anyone, only rival yobs. I'd become an animal. No one at work was aware of my activities. As far as they were concerned I was a good lad who kept his head down. In many ways I did but come Saturday, I'd dive in and help out in the only way I knew how: using my fists. Looking back, I'm not proud of it yet, despite the violence, the fans still had a 'code of conduct'. We never picked on rival fans for wearing the wrong scarf or top and we never hurt women or went near family groups; we only hit thugs who enjoyed a pint and a punch up. It sounds grim but this was the mid-80s when football hooliganism was at its peak.

Despite my alter ego, at work things were going from strength to strength. My boss gave me more responsibility and now, instead of being stuck inside the storeroom all day, I was out in vans with the other full-timers. Brian got me to do industrial cleaning and my wages almost doubled to £70 a week. I was 18 years old and felt like king of the world. It should have been an exciting time only things at home still weren't so good.

Anthony was still dressed in hand-me-downs and so started nicking my new clothes. I'd often find them worn, dirty and sometimes damaged. I went mad but he didn't care because Anthony was turning into a mini version of me. I presumed if I gave him a nice bedroom he'd show more respect, but I was wrong. Our bedroom was grim so I spent £90 doing it up, even splashing out on a new carpet but it didn't stay that way. Anthony, like the rest of us, wasn't used to having nice things and so when he burnt a hole with a cigarette in the bedroom carpet I completely lost it. A row erupted and Dad got involved but instead of Anthony getting it in the neck, I did. Nothing had changed. Even with my new job, wages, and fancy clothes, I was and always would be the black sheep of the family. Grabbing my stuff I stormed out of the house and ran down to nearby woods. I undid the tin in my hand and calmly watched as the needle punctured my skin. I injected a week's worth of insulin in just one hit and within minutes the rush caused me to go hypo. My blood sugar was at an all time low – I knew I was in danger. It was a stupid thing to do, it had been a cry for help but now I was frightened. I didn't want to die, I was only 18. My body swayed around like an alcoholic who'd had too much to drink as my mind became scrambled and disorientated. Somehow I made it back to the main road and staggered on until I reached the edge of the estate where I stopped a passing man.

'Can you call an ambulance?' I gasped before collapsing in front of him onto the pavement.

Minutes later I heard a wailing siren. I blinked as flashing blue lights approached and someone lifted me up onto a stretcher. I was taken to Bristol's Frenchay Hospital, where doctors put me on a glucose drip to sort my blood sugar levels out. Although no one said anything directly to me, the nurses weren't sympathetic and rightly so; I'd done it to myself. The following day I felt utterly ashamed and, as soon as I was able to stand, I signed myself out.

Despite being desperately weak, I went to work as normal where I made an excuse and hid at the back of the storeroom for the rest of the day. As afternoon crept in, I couldn't face going home so I pulled up a few boxes, dragged out an old sheet and made up a makeshift bed. I hid it away in the corner. There was a packet of biscuits on the side so I knew I'd have enough sugary snacks to see me through the night. Brian didn't know I was there and, if he had I'd have been sacked on the spot. Instead, I locked the door from the inside and kept quiet. I glanced down at my watch, almost 7pm, everyone would be gone by now. I put my ear against the door and listened, it was silent. Flicking on the light, I pulled out my cassette player and pressed play. Music flooded the room and I immediately felt better. I lived in the storeroom for a few days but I was so frightened of losing my job that I swallowed my pride and returned home. My parents smirked as soon as they saw me.

'Knew you'd come crawling back,' Mum sniffed.

I hung up my jacket and went straight to my room.

Despite my tough image, the girls in the neighbourhood seemed to like the fact that I was a bit of a bad lad. I started going out with a girl called Lorraine. I really liked Lorraine and I knew she was keen on me; just being with her brightened my day. One afternoon, Lorraine phoned the house asking for me. I heard the phone ringing but Mum reached it before I did. When she heard Lorraine's voice, she went ballistic.

'Don't you ever give this telephone number out to anyone,' she hissed throwing the receiver at me.

I was mortified.

'Umm, sorry,' Lorraine apologised.

'No, it's fine, honestly,' I told her. 'She's just in a bad mood.'

Thankfully, it didn't put her off, but weeks later when she knocked at the door, my parents made her feel so unwelcome that she never came back again.

Life continued in a blur of work and football but on Valentine's Day 1986, something happened which changed everything. That day I was busy in the storeroom but had the radio blaring away in the background. Suddenly, a news bulletin came on; a young motorcyclist had been killed in an accident in Frampton Cotterell. Lots of my mates drove motorcycles but there was one in particular on my mind and his name was Shaun. He loved his bike; it was his pride and joy. I prayed to God it wasn't him.

I threw down the box in my hands and ran out of the storeroom to look for Brian. He was busy at his desk looking through a pile of order forms but glanced up as soon as he saw me burst through the door.

'Can I use the phone in the office? It's really urgent.'

Brian nodded; he could tell by the look on my face it was something serious.

'What's wrong John?'

'Nothing, hopefully,' I shouted as I ran towards the main office and the phone. My hand was shaking as I picked up the receiver and dialled a number. It took an age for someone to answer but finally a voice on the other end of the line spoke.

'Mum, it's John. There's been a motorbike accident. It's not Shaun, is it?'

Mum listened on the other end of the line, paused and then replied.

'Yeah, yeah, it's him. It's Shaun.' There wasn't an ounce of emotion in her voice.

Nausea rose inside me. I clasped a hand over my mouth and dropped the receiver as if it had just bitten me. A lady who worked in the office heard every word and came running over. She made me a cuppa and led me outside to some steps where I held the hot mug of tea in my trembling hands. I opened up and began to cry, I was absolutely heartbroken. Shaun was just 19.

In the days that followed I struggled to take it all in, Shaun's death was the second loss I'd suffered in as many years; both were good lads but both had been taken. A week later I attended Shaun's funeral along with a bunch of others from my council estate. We climbed onto a minibus but the atmosphere on board was sober as everyone was lost in their own thoughts. We were halfway to the crematorium when the minibus spluttered and slowed, eventually coming to a halt at the side of the road. The driver threw his arms up in the air in total dismay.

'Right, everybody off,' he announced pulling open the door.

'What? But the crem's half a mile away.' I gasped.

'I know it is,' he replied, 'but the minibus has broken down so we're gonna have to make the rest of the way by foot.'

I glanced at my watch: only ten minutes until the ceremony. I jumped up, headed through the door and started to run. Everyone had the same idea and soon a dozen of us were tearing down the main road towards the crematorium. We must have looked a sight, dressed in our funeral attire. Just then, I heard someone coughing at the back of the group, it was the driver. I hadn't realised but he was one of the mourners too, no wonder he'd seemed so stressed. By now he was purple in the face, huffing and puffing just trying to keep up.

Thankfully, we made it with just seconds to spare. I was still gasping for air when I took my seat at the back of the service. I glanced around and grinned, we all looked red-faced, sweating and knackered. I allowed myself a little chuckle because I knew that Shaun would've laughed his socks off.

The service was packed and extremely moving but it felt so wrong. Young people should never die before their time, especially not someone like Shaun. After the service we wandered outside to where his family was waiting. I spotted Shaun's older brother Gary first. He looked so devastated that I wanted to reach out and hug him or wrap a reassuring arm around him, but blokes didn't do stuff like that. Instead we stood there in silence. The rest of Shaun's family passed by but I didn't say a word because I didn't want to intrude. It all felt so stiff and awkward. Shaun's death shook me and made me question why it'd been him and not me. Why had I been allowed to live when good blokes like Shaun and Lee were dead? Nothing seemed to make much sense. When I received my next wage packet, I blew the lot on booze in a bid to ease the pain. I was angry at everything, especially life.

In true haphazard style, I owned and drove a car even though I hadn't had a single lesson or passed my driving test. I bought a bright yellow Cortina off a bloke for a bargain £400, and was delighted when he agreed to let me pay it off in instalments. I only held a provisional licence at that time but shamefully, it didn't stop me from getting behind the wheel, although driving a sunshine yellow car meant I didn't go unnoticed by the local police who pulled me over many times. Obviously, I gave them a false name and address but they finally caught up with me and I landed in trouble once more. I finally passed my driving test at the age of 24, but it was after years of driving illegally, putting both myself and everyone else at risk, but I was selfish sod.

Days later, I got into a fight with a local enemy. I was driving past when he stuck two fingers up at me so I slammed the brakes on, got out of the car and gave him a good pasting. He went straight to the police and I was arrested within the hour and charged with ABH. But it was a Saturday, so the police held me in cells over the weekend until my court appearance on Monday. All morning, I watched the clock. I needed to be at work, but 8.30am came and went. I was stuck there until court started at 10am. A few hours later, the magistrate bailed me. Afterwards, I ran straight to work because I knew I had to tell Brian before anyone else did. I expected to get the sack but Brian was a better man than me.

'I'll come with you next time you're up and I'll vouch for you,' he offered. 'Tell them what a good worker you are. I don't want to lose you.'

My wonderful boss offered to do all that for me even though he'd since discovered that I'd lied to him over my schooling. He was such a decent bloke; he was still willing to give me another chance.

'Just keep this clean and you'll be okay,' he said tapping the side of his nose.

Three weeks later and true to his word, Brian accompanied me to court. His eyes widened a little when he heard it was my fourth ABH conviction, but he stood his ground and gave me a glowing character reference. Thanks to him, I escaped prison by the skin of my teeth. I vowed to make it up to him and, for a while I did but in the end I buggered it up as usual.

My monthly wage seemed to drain through my fingers and by week two, I'd always be skint. I took a second job cleaning windows, anything to earn a few extra few bob, but the money burned a hole in my pocket and never lasted.

That weekend Bristol City were playing away but I couldn't afford a ticket. I should have known better, but I was stupid and selfish so I turned to theft.

A few days later, I was asked to travel along with two colleagues to a local chocolate factory. It was a big on-going contract and we'd been asked to clean the machinery. But instead of doing what I was told my eyes darted everywhere trying to work out what I could steal. As we parked up the van in the loading bay I spotted a pile of aluminium trays to the side. There were dozens of them all battered and smashed up. They looked like rubbish but I knew they had scrap metal value. As luck would have it, our van was parked right next to them so, by the end of the shift, I casually loaded 24 trays into the back and slammed the door. I later sold them for scrap – for the princely sum of £30 – more than enough for a football ticket. Unbeknown to me, someone at the factory had seen it and reported me. His version was backed up by one of my colleagues in the van. When Brian found out he went mental. I felt like scum because I'd betrayed his trust even though he'd been the only person to ever stick up for me. Now I couldn't even stand myself.

'Why John?' Brian said, demanding an answer.

But I didn't have one. I did it and I deserved to be punished. In the end, he sacked me on the spot. With no job, and theft charge hanging over my head, my folks kicked me out too. I started sleeping rough. Sometimes I'd get lucky and land a night on friend's sofa, but I always outstayed my welcome. I was a selfish little twat and now I was getting my comeuppance. I appeared in court where I pleaded guilty to theft and was given two years probation and a hefty fine. I vowed never to steal anything ever again and, from that moment on, I never did.

In a bid to get my life back on track I held down a few labouring jobs, eventually securing a full-time job in a slaughterhouse. It was grim work but at least it was an honest wage. However, just three months later the firm went bust and I was back on my arse again.

My behaviour spiralled out of control. I lashed out at the world and got caught up in various fights. One day I was arrested and remanded in custody charged with affray. One bout of trouble followed another and sometimes, for a quiet life and a warm cell bed, I'd admit to crimes I hadn't even committed. With no income I lived hand-to-mouth, drifting from one odd job to another just to survive. I slept rough in bike sheds, garages, even by the river. But fate was about to give me another chance. I didn't know it then but I was about to meet the love of my life.

CHAPTER NINE

Top Girl

M Y SISTER CLAIR couldn't stand seeing me homeless and so offered to put me up on her sofa. It was a kind gesture and one she repeated many times over the years. Clair had moved out of the family home, given birth to a son and managed to secure a place of her own so she wanted to help.

'It's not much, only a sofa but at least it'll give you a roof over your head,' she insisted, throwing me a duvet.

'Thanks,' I replied as I bedded down for the night.

I knew I didn't deserve Clair's or anyone else's kindness. I was 20 now and had no job, a criminal record and a temporary roof over my head. I was hardly a catch, yet fate had other plans.

A month after moving in, I nipped out to the newsagents to buy a daily paper. I'd been out the night before so I was feeling rough and a little hung over. I'd almost stayed in bed that day but there was a book serialisation in the paper I wanted to read. As I left the shop, I opened it up and was flicking through when I heard someone wolf-whistle behind me. I looked up but no one else was there, someone was wolf-whistling me! I turned around and saw two girls propped up against the wall both giggling away. One in particular caught my eye; she was short and petite with cropped dark spiky hair and very pretty. With nothing to lose I sauntered over to introduce myself.

'Hello,' I began. 'What's your name?' I directed my question at the pretty girl.

'Tracey,' she replied.

'I'm John. So, do you live round here?'

As the conversation flowed I made it clear that I liked Tracey. I dropped hint after hint for her mate to bugger off but she just followed us as we walked along by the river.

'So,' I said. 'What music are you into Tracey?' I could tell by her clothes and hair that she wasn't into the usual rubbish.

'Billy Idol,' she grinned. I nodded my head in approval. Billy had been lead singer with Generation X, and a leading punk so he was okay in my book. I watched her face light up as soon as she started talking about music. I knew she was a woman after my own heart. Soon we were chatting away like old friends and I didn't want to say goodbye.

'Here,' Tracey said, pulling out a pen and scrap of paper. 'Here's my telephone number, give me a ring.'

'I will,' I grinned back. 'I'll guard this number with my heart,' I joked holding it to my chest. I wanted to kiss her goodbye but her friend was watching and I felt too uncomfortable.

'I'll see you soon,' Tracey said waving goodbye.

'You will,' I insisted. 'And I'll ring you, promise!'

But when I appeared in court the following Monday, the judge sent me to jail for 12 months for breaching my ABH probation order. Part of my probation was to sign in and attend regular awareness classes. I thought they were a complete waste of time so I didn't bother and now it'd cost me my freedom. I was taken to a holding cell and put on a prison van bound for Pucklechurch, a youth remand centre. My behaviour became so disruptive that I was moved to other prisons and finally ended up in Cardiff. Being one of the few English blokes amongst a prison full of proud Welshmen was tough. I was targeted because of my nationality, but the truth of it was I didn't feel anymore English than they did. I was a loner who didn't belong anywhere. Once again, my reputation preceded me and I was put into solitary confinement. I just couldn't behave myself; I antagonised the staff and wound them up so much that I was in and out of that cell constantly over three months. It was rough but I was used to my own company. I served my time although I often thought about Tracey and what she might be up to. In the end, I decided it was probably best all round if I forgot about her, besides, she was far too good for me. Towards the end of my sentence I returned to Pucklechurch, which seemed a doddle after Cardiff. With only weeks left to go, I was given a job on reception. I worked so hard that one of the staff organised for me to move into a B&B and attend a college course on my release. I was grateful: maybe there was hope for me after all. With everything in place, I looked forward to my release date, however just days before it came I was called over by one of the guards.

'You've got a visitor,' he informed me.

I was puzzled. I hadn't applied for any visitors passes and so didn't have a clue who it could be. I walked towards the room with a little trepidation. I was worried it was the police. One of my biggest fears was a 'gate arrest', where you get arrested just before your release. My mind thought back to all the trouble I'd been involved in over the years.

Had I missed something?

I wouldn't know for sure until I opened the door. As soon as I did my feet were rooted to the spot. It wasn't the police after all, but Mum. I was absolutely flabbergasted. As I sat down opposite her I couldn't help but stare because she had tears in her eyes. She dabbed at them with a soggy tissue as she spoke.

'Come home John,' she begged.

My mouth hung open with shock. It was weird enough seeing Mum cry but to hear her asking me home was even more astonishing. It took me a few minutes but I gathered my composure and answered.

'I can't come home, how can I?'

Surely it was obvious, even to Mum, who lived in a world of her own, but my words made her sob more.

'Anyway,' I said, 'they've sorted me out with a place to live and I'm going to college.' Excitement rose in my voice as I spoke, I was really looking forward to my new start.

'But it'll be different, I promise. Please come home.'

I looked at her and my heart lurched. She'd come here to ask me back yet, all I could do was think of myself, I was a selfish and horrible person. If I was going to change then I needed to start right now.

'Okay,' I nodded. 'I'll come home.'

Mum smiled as if I'd just made her day and it lifted my heart. Maybe she wasn't so bad after all?

My prison worker was disappointed when I told her that I wouldn't be going to college.

'I'm going home,' I insisted and, for the first time in my life, I felt wanted. It was a good feeling. However, if I thought my Mum wanted or needed me I was sadly mistaken. Within days of returning home the same old rows started and, when I asked for a key to the front door all I got was a load of abuse. In the end, I gave up and stormed out.

'Where do you think you're going?' she cried after me down the street.

'I'm off out to see my mates,' I snapped.

Nothing had changed.

'Well I want you back by 10pm.'

'Christ, I'm 21 years old!'

Looking back, I think she did it on purpose, to scupper my chance at a new life. She didn't care.

When I returned later that evening she'd locked the door from the inside. It had gone 10pm, so she'd shut me out. With nowhere else to go, I slept inside my car.

A few days later, I was going through my jacket when I found the crumpled piece of paper with Tracey's number written on it. I put it down on the table and stared at it.

Sod it, I thought. *Nothing ventured, nothing gained.*

I snatched it back up and stuffed it inside my pocket. Running downstairs, I slammed the door behind me and walked along the street, towards the phone box. I spotted a familiar figure up ahead. I recognised the jacket and the dark spiky hair, it was Tracey.

'I was just gonna call you,' I said grinning from ear to ear. It sounded corny but it was true.

'Yeah, sure,' she smirked.

'No, honestly, look!' I said holding the piece of paper up in my hand to prove the point. Tracey grinned and blushed a little. I took it as a good sign; she still liked me.

'So, where have you been hiding?' she asked. She was as lovely and pretty as I remembered.

I thought about making up some fancy story but Tracey was a smart cookie and she'd soon see straight through it. Besides, everyone in the neighbourhood knew what I was like so she probably already knew.

'I've been banged up,' I admitted staring down at my boots. Tracey went quiet but I knew she'd done her homework, I wasn't snow white and she knew it.

'What for?'

'I breached my probation,' I replied honestly. 'But I missed you.'

Her face lit up. Most girls would've run a mile at this point and rightly so but not Tracey. As luck would have it, she liked naughty boys and I was certainly one of them. We started seeing one another and things soon became serious.

A few weeks later, Tracey invited me back to hers to meet her parents. She proudly held my hand as we approached her front door. As soon as I saw it I felt nervous and out of my depth because it was a big posh house with a lovely neat clipped garden. I knew that I didn't belong. My nerves gave way to something else and I immediately went on the defensive. Despite my obnoxious manner, Tracey's parents were extremely welcoming and, if they were disappointed, they never let it show. Originally from Yorkshire, Trevor and

Jackie were lovely, down-to-earth, hardworking folks who just wanted the best for their daughter. God only knows what they thought when they saw me coming through the door. Whatever their reservations they never once bad-mouthed me or treated me with anything but respect. Trevor worked as a manager for British Gas, whilst Jackie worked as a medical records officer at a nearby hospital. Unlike my house, Tracey's was immaculate and full of lovely things. It was clear they'd worked hard for everything they had – they were the total opposite of me.

Despite having a lovely girlfriend, I was still in and out of court for various misdemeanours. If I thought my criminal activities were something I could keep it to myself, I was sorely mistaken because I was always in the local paper.

Tracey's parents must have known but they chose not to bring it up at the dinner table. I was relieved because I didn't feel worthy of being in their house, never mind dating their beautiful daughter. I think they thought our relationship would fizzle out but it never did. Instead, I tried my best to smarten up my act, after all I had Tracey to look after now. But however I dressed myself up I was still a selfish git. Although I took Tracey to watch football in a bid to keep me out of trouble, if a fight broke out I'd just abandon her in the stands so I could go and join in. Looking back, I don't know how she put up with me.

After four months together, we announced our engagement. If her family were horrified, they never let it slip. We held a party in a local pub and all my mates and family came – everyone apart from Mum. They all presumed we'd enjoy a long engagement but they were wrong because, just a few months later, in March 1990, we nipped into Bristol Register office and became Mr and Mrs Tovey. We knew our families wouldn't approve so we didn't tell a soul. It was a selfish and reckless thing to do but I didn't care because I loved Tracey more than I'd ever loved anyone. We honeymooned in Paris, but finally returned home to face the music. Of course, her parents were devastated. Tracey had two brothers but she was their only daughter. I realised what I'd done and tried my best to prove I was worthy of her.

With no money saved for a place of our own, I went to live in a nearby hostel while Tracey held down a job working for an insurance company and lived at home with her parents. Even though I was at the hostel, as a married man, I was given my own room complete with a double bed. I kept it spic and span because Tracey would come and stay the night. One day she told me she thought she was pregnant.

'But I need to go to the doctor's and have a proper test,' she explained.

I nodded my head as I tried to contain the butterflies rising inside the pit of my stomach. A few days later I was at the hostel when Tracey walked in.

'I'm pregnant!' she squealed.

I was ecstatic and hugged her for all I was worth. It was all I'd ever wanted, to be a good dad. Tracey's parents accepted the news well but I half expected her brothers to come looking for me, even though we were married!

I was thrilled at the prospect of becoming a dad and was determined my child wouldn't make the same mistakes I had. It made me even more focused on getting a job but with no real skills or qualifications it was tough. Eventually, I landed a position working inside a distribution centre that dispatched goods to one of the main supermarkets. The work was boring and monotonous and, to make things worse, I had to work alongside a big mouthy bloke who took great pleasure in belittling others and who loved to throw his weight around. For the first few months, I kept my head down but I soon tired of his bullying ways.

One day I was at work when I heard a noise behind me. I turned to see a forklift truck hurtling straight at me. Suddenly I had a flashback of Lee, the digger and the accident. My heart was in my mouth as I jumped clear just in time.

'Careful!' I shouted to the driver who turned and that's when I realised it was him, the big mouthy bastard, behind the wheel.

I knew by the look on his face that this had been no accident; he'd done it to freak me out. My blood boiled as he climbed down from the cab of the truck and I watched as he strode across the factory towards the gents toilets. I quickened my pace as I balled my fists in preparation. I shoved the door open so hard that it banged against the wall loudly. The fat bastard was at the sink washing his porky little hands. I smacked him against the side of his head and he immediately went down as heavy as a sack of potatoes. I was astonished how such a big, fat bully could fall so easily.

'If you ever do that to me again, I'll kill you,' I said.

I was so angry that I hissed the words through gritted teeth. A rage fired up inside me but somehow I turned, walked away and went back to work. Moments later, two security guards hovered over me. The weasely bastard had reported me to management and, despite everything he'd done over the years, I was the one who got the sack.

I managed to get myself another job and tried my best to change my ways. I stopped going to football altogether in a bid to stay out of trouble. A reformed man, I went out and bought a cage and a couple of canaries. After that I devoted all my time to breeding the beautiful little creatures. I became so obsessed that I was known as the Bird Man of Alcatraz!

Our beautiful son James was born in May 1991, and with a young baby to look after, we managed to secure a council flat in Frampton Cotterell when James was seven months old. However Tracey wasn't keen.

'Are you sure you want to move back there?' she asked.

I nodded my head.

'I'm certain.'

But in the end, Tracey was right. I thought it'd be a fresh move and a new start but with my demons from my past haunting me, it turned out to be the biggest mistake of my life.

I stopped drinking and tried to become the best dad in the world. I'd finally arrived and, despite being a little sod all my life, I'd somehow managed to marry the prettiest girl in town, get my own place and be blessed with a son. With my life on the up, I even tried to rebuild my fractured relationship with my family, particularly my parents. I was a grown man with responsibilities but if I'd hoped that would win their seal of approval I was wrong. Even though I helped them out doing odd jobs, I was always seen as the thorn in Mum's side.

In 1992, a mate knocked at my door.

'Here, John, have you heard? Madness are reforming.'

'What?' I said, thinking he was taking the piss.

But he wasn't. Months later in August, I found myself at the front of the stage at Madstock with hundreds of other

Dez starting out
on his Guide Dog
adventure.

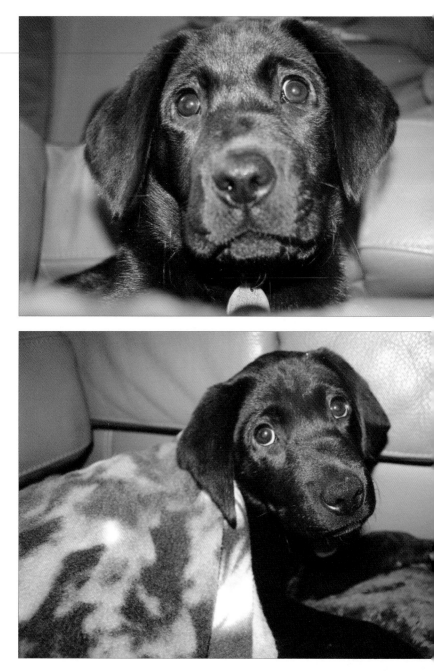

Settling into life with his puppy walkers, who looked after Dez at the puppy walking stage.

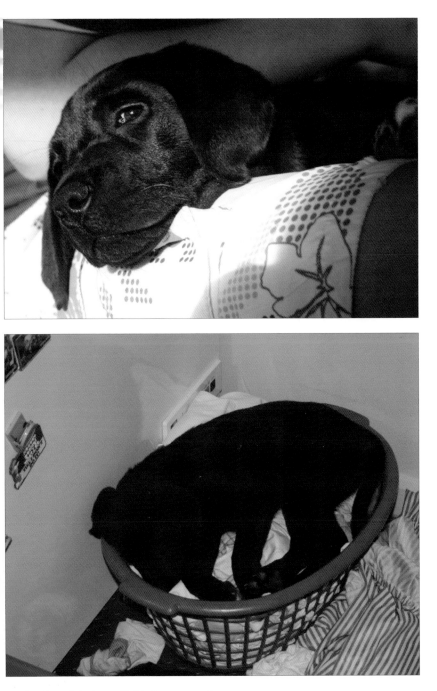

It's hard work being a Guide Dog puppy!

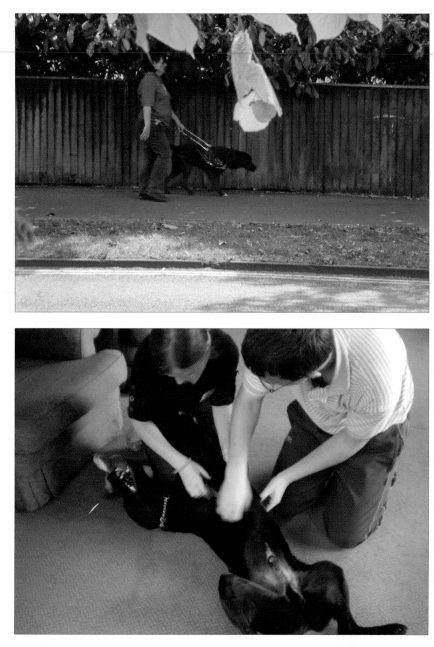

Above: Dez in training.

Below: Taking a well-deserved break from learning the skills needed to become a fully-fledged Guide Dog.

All part of the training: Dez meets a friend that looks a bit like him!

Above: Guide Dogs have to look their best!

Below: Dez with puppy walkers, the Greensills.

All grown up: Dez is ready
to meet his new owner.

Above: Best friends.

Below: Dez wins the 2012 Guide Dog of the Year award.

nutters. Even though I was dancing it felt as if I was floating on air. It was a red hot day and I was there, once again with the best band in the world. The crowd was riotous but everyone was in good spirits.

Tracey stayed at home with James, so I went along with my mates Phil and Mick, and danced like I'd never danced before. I pissed myself laughing the following day when I read how the crowd had stomped so hard that it'd been recorded as a small earthquake in the Finsbury Park area of London. But that's Madness for you!

My son was the centre of my life. As he grew I taught him how to play cricket and he became so good that he joined Winterbourne Cricket Club. He was only eight years old but he often played alongside children much older. Some of my happiest days were spent standing on the sidelines watching him be the boy I'd always wanted to be. Members of the club welcomed me with open arms but I felt ashamed and embarrassed by my chequered past. I worried that it would somehow tarnish my talented little boy. I chose to keep my distance from the other parents. I eyed them along on the sideline and even recognised a few I'd walloped over the years. Yet, despite everything, they tried their best to encourage James. I was the ultimate proud father and, against all odds, I'd managed to produce an amazing kid.

Although I loved Tracey with all my heart, my upbringing meant I found it difficult to show love. Despite having the best wife a man could ever wish to have, I was cold and unloving and pushed my lovely Tracey away. I didn't understand why I was like I was, unable to give or receive love. My head was plagued by my troubled past. Whenever

Tracey came near, I'd shrink away back into my own world. She offered me love but I felt suffocated by it. Physically, I couldn't bear to be touched. I'd got everything I'd ever wanted but now I was slowly destroying it all, piece by piece. My past had never really gone away. Instead it was still there, slowly strangling me. It refused to let me move on or be happy and now I couldn't and didn't know how to let anyone in. Instead of talking about it, I bottled everything up and turned to the only thing that brought me comfort: drink. Tracey tried her best to help but selfishly I refused to listen to her or anyone else. I realised I'd spent most of my childhood alone. I was a lone wolf who really didn't know how to love or live inside a happy family unit. It was all I'd ever wanted, but try as I might, I just couldn't do it. Slowly but surely, our marriage broke down.

In a bid to escape, Tracey took James to her parents for the weekend. She needed to get away from me. She'd been good for me and, although I loved her with all my heart, I was too selfish to let her go. Instead, I lived with the daily fear that she would leave, but she didn't and somehow we stuck together.

I held down a job as a maintenance man at a big hotel in Bath and when a young girl started to pay me attention, I felt flattered. Soon we were having an affair. It was the classic younger woman scenario. I was only 28 but felt stuck – I was looking for an escape. If truth be told, so was Tracey. Working in a hotel offered me the perfect opportunity to stay over and sleep in the staff accommodation. I don't know why I did it. Perhaps, subconsciously I was trying to force Tracey away? Or perhaps I was just a complete and utter shit. Whatever it was, Tracey certainly didn't deserve it or me.

She never found out but instead of leaving for good, I took the coward's way out and got a job working away.

I'd drifted in and out of employment so, when a friend mentioned they were looking for men to work on the Channel Tunnel, I jumped at the chance. The tunnel needed to be excavated to allow trains to travel under the sea from Kent to France. The whole idea sounded a little sci-fi and crazy at the time but I was told there was good money to be made so I packed a bag and went.

I left Bristol in 1994, and at first, I worked away for a week or two at a time. I started as surface labourer just sweeping and moving rubbish around. It was boring and monotonous but all the lads on site travelled to work there so, in many ways, it reminded me a little of prison. The harder I worked the more responsibility and training I was given. Eventually, I secured a job working on the Jubilee Line extension and the Docklands Light Railway in London, both of which were being developed. The job meant more money but it also meant long periods of time away from home.

Every evening after work, the lads would meet up and head down the pub for a pint but I didn't. Instead, I shut myself off and chose to drink alone. At weekends I'd hop on a train to go back to see James. Yet, despite my role as a doting father, by the end of the weekend I'd be itching to get back to London so I could drink some more. I didn't realise it but I was slowly drinking myself to death. On a few occasions I even got into fights with colleagues. A few times I got the sack but I'd just travel across London to pick up a new job.

After almost 11 years of marriage, Tracey realised we couldn't go on like this and ended it. I shook my head in despair – I'd done it – I'd finally destroyed everything I loved. I begged Tracey to come back and even promised I'd change but she knew I couldn't. I'd put Tracey up on a pedestal and when we split it was as though my whole world had come crashing down.

Despite my plans to give my son the best childhood ever, I became a part-time dad, taking him to the park to play cricket. The truth was, I'd neglected them both and now I was paying a high price for my stupidity. I was an idiot. I'd had everything but I'd thrown it all away and the most ridiculous part of it all was that I didn't even know why.

CHAPTER TEN

Journey to Hell

I MOVED TO LONDON permanently in the autumn of the new millennium. For many it was a new start and in a way it was for me too. This was my life now.

Armed with a bulging wage packet, I'd send a chunk back to Tracey for James and booze the rest up the wall. I was high on beer with whisky and vodka chasers. My drinking became so bad that soon I was buying half a bottle of vodka just to drink on my way to the pub. The years passed by in a blur of routine, work, drink and journeys home to see my son. I was drinking every single day, sometimes up to a whole bottle of whisky. I'd pressed the self-destruct button and was now well on the way to ruin.

My home was a small flat in the Canning Town area of London. By day, I worked at the Canary Wharf development, mainly on the HSBC tower. There was lots of on-going investment in the city and for someone in my job as a fabricator and welder there was a lot of money to be made. Soon I was cash rich and, when James was 12, I had enough in the bank to send him to private school. But I refused to let him board, he was always a day pupil. I was determined he'd get a good education and not follow the same path I did. I wanted James to have aspirations and expect more from life than his old man ever had.

Tracey and I had split but before then we had upgraded to a nice three-bed semi-detached house in Sunnyside, Frampton Cotterell, so she stayed there whilst I remained holed up in London. We talked often on the phone, mainly about James, and vowed to remain friends for his sake. Tracey was and still is a good person and just because things hadn't worked out between us didn't mean I wanted to lose my best friend. There was no massive row or bust-up, I'd seen too many in my youth; instead we decided to deal with it like adults. I still loved my ex-wife but I knew I couldn't make her happy and that was the one thing she deserved more than anything else in the world. So, I was delighted for her when a few years later she met a lovely bloke called Phil. Together they went onto marry and have two beautiful daughters. Despite everything, we all remained friends so much so, that as soon as the girls were born, I became their unofficial uncle – a title I still hold proud to this day.

Work on the Channel Tunnel rail link started up so I got a job working on a tunnel boring machine. It was hard and dirty graft but the money was plentiful as we slowly bored our way through the city from St Pancras to Kent. Now and again, work would dry up and we'd get laid off between contracts. But instead of hanging around I'd just go out and look for other work to keep the money coming in for James's schooling.

It was during one of our contract breaks that I was asked to construct a plant room –basically a building on top of a building – for a friend of a friend. I worked hard on the project and expected good recompense but when the time came to hand over the job to the client he suddenly started finding fault in my work and was reluctant to hand over the cash. He became difficult and aggressive but I needed the money to pay for James's education and when he refused to pay I lost my temper. We started to fight but I completely lost it. A rage took over me and before I realised, I'd beaten the man to a pulp. Physically, he was much bigger but I made a real mess of him and was so out of control that my work colleagues had to drag me off. The police were called and I was charged with GBH. Even though I'd been clean for a while, with my previous convictions, they threw the book at me. I'd messed up again.

In the meantime, another contract started up again but I was so terrified of losing my job that I kept quiet about the fight. However, with my impending court appearance I knew the judge was going to have a field day when he saw me in the dock so I did the decent thing and came clean with my boss. I loved my job and, until now, had always kept my head down so when I finally confessed what I'd done, he was flabbergasted.

'What you up for John? Driving offences?' he asked.

'No, fighting,' I confessed.

He looked at me a little shocked and then burst out laughing. No one in London knew about my dark past so at first he didn't believe me.

'Yeah, right, pull the other one,' he laughed, throwing his head back. He pointed his finger at me in jest. 'You're good, you know that? You almost had me going there for a minute.'

'It's true.' I insisted.

He looked up and shook his head.

It sounds odd but because I'd kept my slate clean no one in London saw me as a troublemaker. I'd managed to reinvent myself and build a whole new life but now it had come tumbling down. He listened intently as I explained what had happened and how I needed the money to pay for James's schooling.

'I just want him to have a better life than me.' I explained.

'I'll tell you what,' he said finally. 'If you get sent down, I promise that I'll keep your job open. You're a good worker John, I don't want to lose you.'

I thanked him. At least I knew I'd have a job waiting for me.

I appeared at Middlesex Guildhall Crown Court, where I pleaded not guilty for the first time in my life because I truly believed that I'd acted in self-defence. In the end, I had two trials; the first resulted in a hung jury, whilst the second saw a majority decision. Although the court accepted some of my defence the letter of the law ruled that I'd used unreasonable force and so I was convicted and sentenced to 18 months' imprisonment. I'd gambled with my freedom, not for the first time and now, like a big game of snakes and ladders, I'd just slipped right down to the beginning again.

I served half my sentence, with seven months in Wandsworth prison and the last seven weeks at Ford Open Prison. Wandsworth was hellish – the stuff of nightmares. I didn't want James to visit me there so I tried to keep in contact over the phone. We were locked up for a majority of the time so I was lucky if I was able to speak to him once every fortnight. Sometimes they'd tell us we could only make a call halfway through the day so, with James at school, I'd call Tracey or her parents just to keep my spirits up. Thankfully, Ford Open Prison was a much better place. There I was able to call James every single day. I became a wheeler dealer when it came to phone cards so I always had enough credit to make a call. I even joined the prison cricket team so my last few weeks passed quickly.

True to his word, my old boss kept my job open for me so I literally came out on the Friday and went back to work on Monday. I realised what a lucky sod I was to have such an understanding manager and I vowed to pay him back by working all the hours I could. A few weeks later, I was asked to put in some overtime. They needed a volunteer to go and take some measurements up at Caledonian Road, where the tunnel was breaking through into an alleyway over ground. Keen to show him that he'd made the right decision, I put my hand up.

'Good man, John,' he said.

I couldn't believe it when I arrived at the entrance to the site at Caledonian Road. Right opposite was a phone box which had featured in the Madness documentary film *Take It Or Leave It*. It was an iconic symbol to any Madness fan, so I nipped over and stood inside like a loon, taking it all in. People passing by must have wondered what the hell I was doing gazing all around me inside a phone box but it had been an unexpected bonus and a lovely coincidence. I pretty much knew London like the back of my hand so I was amazed that I'd never thought to visit there before.

By this time I'd moved from my flat in Canning Town to

Stratford so, after I'd packed up my things I boarded a train back home. I was miles away, lost in my own thoughts when I heard my phone bleep in the pocket of my jeans. I took it out to have a look who was texting but as I did, I felt a slight punch to the side of head. It was so pathetic that at first I thought it was someone mucking about but when I looked up I saw two teenagers hovering over me. For a moment I was baffled, but before I had time to react one of the kids leaned forward and snatched my mobile phone.

'Hey!' I shouted.

One of them punched me but I shoved him away. I didn't want any trouble. Then, without warning, the carriage door burst open and within minutes I was surrounded by a gang of them, only these lads were much older and tougher. I thought I was dead. I looked to my fellow passengers but they just buried their heads in their newspapers and tried to ignore what was happening.

There was a blur of angry faces as a gang of about 25 blokes came charging right at me. I waited to get stabbed but thankfully, I wasn't. Instead I was beaten and punched within an inch of my life. I don't know if it was fear or survival instinct but adrenalin kicked in and somehow kept me on my feet. I knew as soon as I went down on the floor I was as good as a dead man. At one point a few of them jumped onto the seats and started kicking me straight in the head but still I refused to sink to my knees. The pain was so excruciating that I thought I'd die right there and then. There was a bloody great big gang and I was trying to fight them off alone. It took every ounce of strength I had to remain standing but I did. Finally, I think they realised they'd met their match. I was a loony, and fighting had been my way of life until now; they'd just picked on the wrong guy. Battered and bleeding, I screamed at them like a demented animal and they backed off warily.

'Come on then!' I yelled, my eyes wide and bloodied.

My head, torso, arms and legs were all split open and I was trying hard to focus through my right eye but my vision was all blurred. They backed off and as the train pulled into the next station they saw their chance and jumped off. Someone alerted the guard who called an ambulance and I was taken off the train on a stretcher and rushed to a nearby hospital. Amazingly, I didn't have one broken bone in my body although the beating had been so severe that I couldn't move and stayed in hospital for a week.

The police came to visit me straight after. They'd caught my attackers – they knew it was them because they'd found my blood on one of the gang's T-shirts. When the detectives asked me to testify against them I refused because I was reluctant to get involved. But as I lay in my hospital bed I started to reflect. I thought about my life and how I'd messed it all up.

Violence follows me around. If I carry on like this I'm never going to get away from it. I've got to change. Something's got to give.

I was still mulling it over when the police reappeared. They told me I'd not been the only victim on the train; there'd been a woman too. I was appalled because a vulnerable female passenger had been attacked. I knew I had to do the right thing. I'd been a yob all my life but I'd never hit a woman. I knew then that I had to do the right thing; I had to testify.

It was strange standing in the witness box instead of the

145

dock and at one point it felt surreal because it was exactly the same court where I'd been jailed only a year earlier for violence. But now I was here to do the right thing. It was a pivotal moment in my life. The defendants stared straight at me but I held my nerve, stood my ground and told the truth.

The court heard how the gang, called the 'Lords of Stratford Crew', had targeted people on trains, tubes and buses in London. The so-called 'steaming' gang had 'street tags' including names such as Killer, Packman and Driller and the prosecution told the court the gang were in it 'mainly for the kicks and thrills' and that they had punched and kicked their way through a dozen victims over a two-week period. Some victims were even stamped upon and left 'virtually senseless' by the attacks, the jury heard. Five members of the gang were convicted of three counts of conspiracy to rob. Even though they'd used extreme violence I was stunned to hear they'd only stolen minor items such as small change and cigarettes. The judge was so horrified by what he called 'gratuitous violence' that he lifted a ban and ordered four of the gang – all juveniles – to be identified because he wanted to highlight the consequences of such behaviour.

The court was told how I was still unable to see properly since the attack. It was true; my eyesight had suffered as a result, leaving me with almost constant blurred vision in my right eye.

With overwhelming evidence stacked up against them, the gang members were found guilty and jailed for a total of 25 years. I sighed with relief because I felt I'd played my part and helped put the gang behind bars where they belonged.

As things turned out, I'd been the gang's last victim. I was glad that I'd spooked them by fighting back because, as the court heard, they could've killed the next person. But now I was a marked man. I'd switched sides and become a grass. I'd have to keep out of trouble now because no one liked a grass and, if I ended up back inside, I'd be a dead man.

The following year passed by in a bit of a blur in more ways than one. I was still having problems with the vision in my right eye but I ignored it and put it down to the attack and the fact I'd been welding for years. Slowly, I cut myself off from everyone apart from Tracey and James. My parents and I had become estranged and, after yet another big row, I walked away from them and the rest of my family. Instead, I selfishly lived my life alone with work and whisky bottles my only companions.

One day I was at work when my mobile rang, it was my sister Clair; she sounded upset and her voice urgent.

'John, it's Mum,' she blurted out. 'She's really ill. You'd better come home.'

I knew Mum had an on-going lung complaint, she'd had it for ages, and it'd been caused by years of heavy smoking. But Clair told me it had worsened and now Mum was fighting for her life. I asked my eldest sister question after question but she didn't have any answers.

'Just come home John,' she said her voice cracking with emotion. 'She hasn't got long left to live.'

As the call ended a lump formed at the back of my throat. All those wasted years, all those rows and fights. All those years when I'd desperately craved my mother's love. But all those times she'd rejected me. I had so many questions but so little time.

I pulled out a bag from the bottom of my wardrobe and threw some things into it. I knew I had to get home fast. I had to speak to Mum because I wanted to tell her how much I loved her but also I wanted to ask her something: why had she hated me all my life?

CHAPTER ELEVEN

Dark Days

A S SOON AS I arrived at the hospital I knew that Clair hadn't been exaggerating. Mum was terminally ill and clinging onto life. I wanted to sit with her and make her comfortable during her final hours but a selfish part of me also saw this as a last chance to ask her why she'd treated me with such contempt as a child? I was confused and emotional. I needed to make peace with Mum, but I also needed to ask her so I could settle demons from my past.

It was odd sitting in a hospital room together. All those years she'd spent avoiding me and now we were trapped together. I asked a nurse to keep the rest of the family outside in the hospital corridor because I wanted some time alone with her – I needed to sort things out once and for all before it was too late.

Although she'd been emotionally brittle most of her life, Mum had always been physically strong. But now, lying in her hospital bed she looked as fragile and vulnerable as a baby bird. I leaned forward and kissed her to let her know I was there but she didn't say very much. Instead, I sat next to her and mulled over how I'd ask the one question that had been burning inside of me all my life: why didn't she love me? It was a horrible thing to say or think, but it was the ugly truth. She'd made my life a living hell and I needed to know why before it was too late.

'Mum,' I began, trying to find the right words.

She turned to face me but looked disappointed when she opened her eyes and realised I was still there. Rejection twisted inside my stomach like a blunt knife.

'There's something I need to ask you.'

She looked frail and emaciated in her hospital bed but I couldn't help it, I needed to do this so I could make my peace with her before she passed away. Mum blinked at me and waited for me to say what I'd come to say.

'I need to know… I mean, I have to know – what was going on back then, when I was a child? Why did you treat me like that Mum?'

But instead of answering she just sighed and turned her head. My heart sank; she wasn't going to tell me the only thing I needed to know.

'What did I do to you that was so wrong?'

But she didn't want to know. I felt like a bastard, but after all those years of being treated like an outcast I needed, no I *deserved* an answer. All the hurt flowed through my veins and the words came tumbling out of my mouth before I'd even had chance to stop them.

'Are you sure he's my real father?' I said suddenly.

There, I'd said it. There was no going back now. It was the

only thing that made any sense. Maybe I belonged to someone else and that's why Mum had spent her life resenting me? It was the only reason I could think why she hated me so much. Without warning she began to sob. She wailed so loud that the door burst open and the nurse came running in. She checked Mum over and turned to me.

'I think you'd better leave.'

I tried to explain to Mum why I'd asked such a horrible question but she refused to make eye contact. That was it; I'd messed up again. I didn't know how to feel because I was churned up inside with regret, love, and grief. In a haze of tears I stumbled outside where my family were waiting. They'd heard Mum's cries and were furious with me.

What had I said? Why did I always have to be such a bastard?

I refused to answer; instead, I pushed past them all and ran out of the hospital. My heart was tight inside my chest as if I couldn't breathe. I needed to get away, I needed time to think how to make things right again, but I didn't know how. I sought solace in the only thing that had supported me over the years, my friend and confidant: drink. I was well on my way to becoming stinking drunk when my mobile phone rang later that evening. I pulled it out from my jacket pocket and looked at the number but it was one I didn't recognise. My voice slurred as I answered. The caller checked she had the right person before continuing. It was a nurse from the hospital, my mother's health had deteriorated and I needed to get there. I was sat in the bar of a bed and breakfast hotel, about a mile away but I ran the whole way. By the time I reached her hospital room she looked peaceful, as if she was sleeping.

'John,' a nurse whispered from behind, 'your mum is unconscious.'

'But is she going to wake up?' I said, shaking my head. This wasn't happening. 'I need to say sorry, I need to speak to her.'

The nurse couldn't tell me. I was heartbroken. I wanted to tell my mum how sorry I was but now I was frightened it was too late.

'She's very poorly,' the nurse explained, 'but we're doing everything we can to make her comfortable.'

Tears pricked at the back of my eyes and flowed down my cheeks. I wanted to shake Mum from her sleep to tell her how sorry I was. I'd loved and hated her in equal measure over the years, but now I'd left it too late to make amends. My body felt stiff and awkward, crippled with guilt and remorse.

I put my hand to my neck and removed my diabetic tag. I laid it on top of her bedside cabinet and turned to the nurse.

'When she wakes up can you tell her I've been back to see her?' I said pointing towards the tag.

The nurse nodded.

'Please tell her I came back. Please tell her I was here.' I wept.

'I will,' the nurse whispered gently leading me from the room.

I felt sick because I knew I'd left it too late. Hours later, my mother died and, it's to my eternal regret and shame that I never got to put things right. Now I could barely stand myself.

On the day of her funeral I was so ashamed that, in an attempt to block it all out, I went to pub and got so paralytic that I ended up in a row with a close friend. It was so bad I even managed to get myself barred from one of the roughest pubs in Bristol, which is no mean feat.

I staggered along the road but was in such a state that I collapsed unconscious into a ditch. I knew they all hated me for what I'd done but I despised myself even more. As I lay in the ditch looking at the blackened night with its bright stars shining down, I prayed the cold or alcohol poisoning would take me. Everything went black and I passed out. I don't know how long I lay there but when I finally opened my eyes, two figures emerged, a man and a woman, and they were dressed in uniform.

'Wake up mate, you okay?' The man's voice called. I felt someone shake my left shoulder.

'Who's that?' I slurred.

'It's the police.'

Oh God, here we go, I thought. *This is where I get arrested.*

But the police officer seemed more concerned than angry.

'You okay?' he asked again, this time checking me over. 'Are you hurt anywhere?'

'It was my Mum's funeral today.' I wept. Tears dripped off my face as I tried to wipe my eyes with the back of my sleeve but it was no good, I couldn't stop them.

I held out my arms waiting for the familiar feel of metal against skin and chink of handcuffs but instead the officer grabbed my hand and helped me up to my feet.

'Let's get you to the hospital,' his female colleague said, wrapping a reassuring arm around my shoulder to steady me.

'I think we need to get you checked out.'

A short while later I was in A & E at the very same hospital where my mother had passed away. The female officer sat with me whilst her colleague booked me in with the hospital receptionist. By now I'd sobered up enough to know I wasn't going to be arrested. These officers were different to ones I'd encountered before, they were sympathetic and didn't judge me, but treated me with respect and kindness.

A call crackled through on the policeman's radio and soon they had to leave. As they stood up I thanked them for their kindness.

'And don't forget to get yourself checked out now, will you?' the female officer insisted.

'I won't. Thank you.'

I meant every word. They'd both just restored my faith in the police service.

I remained a few minutes longer sat on my plastic chair. My body was pooled in the stark and bright strip lighting of A & E. It was harsh and unforgiving, but it helped me sober up and see things a little clearer. I clambered to my feet and headed out the door. I didn't bother to get checked out, what was the point?

I returned to London where I kept my head down and carried on with my job. Before I knew it, three months had passed by. I cut myself off from everyone, particularly my family, who hated me with good reason.

I started getting chest pains but I ignored them and I told myself it was because I was getting older.

One weekend, I was travelling back on the train to see James when I started to feel really ill. My chest felt so tight that I found it difficult to breathe; I also had vicious pins and needles shooting down my left arm towards my fingers. By the time the train pulled into Bristol, I felt so ill that I dialled for a cab.

'Where to, mate?' The driver asked.

'Frenchay Hospital,' I gasped. 'Accident and Emergency.'

Somehow I staggered inside, grey and sweating profusely. Nausea overwhelmed me as I approached the receptionist and begged for help. Within moments I was in a hospital waiting bay surrounded by a group of doctors. Someone placed some sticky pads across my chest and wheeled in a machine. A nurse injected my stomach with a blood thinning fluid as others quickly got to work on me. A doctor was asking me lots of questions but I could barely think straight as my mind went into a complete panic. After what seemed like an eternity, a consultant came over to speak to me.

'You've had a mild heart attack,' he explained.

I was so stunned that at first I thought I hadn't heard him correctly.

'Me?' I gasped in disbelief. 'Are you sure?'

Since the attack I'd suffered a bit of blurring in my right eye but apart from that, I felt physically fine. But the ECG and subsequent blood tests confirmed I'd had a heart attack and that my heart had suffered some damage. I was a time bomb waiting to happen.

'You need to start looking after yourself,' the doctor told me bluntly as he explained that I needed to be admitted for further tests.

'I can't,' I told him. 'I work in London and I need to get back.'

The doctor refused.

'You need an angiogram Mr Tovey,' he said slowly, as if the message wasn't getting through.

'Okay, but I'll come back for it,' I promised.

Against the doctor's advice I signed myself out of hospital. Staff prescribed me some medication, a follow-up appointment and a spray in case of an angina attack, but I couldn't wait to get out of there.

'I'll be fine,' I insisted as I staggered towards the door.

Only I wasn't. Two weeks later I was back home in Bristol

when exactly the same thing happened again. This time, I was admitted to the coronary care unit, where I remained for a few weeks. I was in a bad way and I knew it. I needed an operation to insert a stent, to help prop open my failing heart. Frightened and alone I underwent the op and I actually felt relieved when I woke up again. I'd survived, but afterwards I felt as if I was living on borrowed time. Every little twinge put me on full alert.

I decided I needed to take control of my life. I'd been in a bad way since Mum's death and even though I'd seen first-hand how cigarettes had stolen her life I was letting history repeat itself. I'd smoked since the age of nine but now I was in my late thirties, and I'd had my warning. It was time to kick the fags. I was a diabetic who drank too much, ate badly and hardly ever slept. If I wanted to get better I needed to get a grip. The doctor was right; I needed to look after myself.

My eyesight was getting worse too. At one point it became so bad that I packed up my bags and moved back to Bristol for a while. I secured a bit of labouring work and tried to clean up my life but there was one thing I just couldn't put right: my fractured relationship with my family.

Then, a year later, in May 2006, I received a phone call that turned my world upside down.

'John,' a voice said on the other end of the phone. I recognised it immediately; it was the husband of a close family friend.

'John, I'm so sorry. I don't know how to tell you this but it's your brother Anthony.'

My ears pricked up at the mention of Anthony's name.

'What about him? What's happened?'

'He's died.'

I almost dropped the phone in shock. Anthony was only 37. I asked questions but the man didn't know much more.

Anthony had been found dead in a house and it looked as if drugs were to blame. Initial tests had shown traces of cocaine and heroin in his blood. I felt responsible. I'd heard a rumour Anthony had been dabbling with drugs so I'd spoken with him to try and shake some sense into him. I thought I had but now, just like Mum, it was too late.

In the days that followed, Anthony's death hit me hard. He'd always been such a lovely, affable guy but also very easily led. We'd spoken when I'd heard he'd been messing around with ecstasy and cocaine but never, in a million years, did I ever think he'd try heroin. But now he had, and it had killed him. If I'd felt guilty over Mum, I felt twice as bad over Anthony. As his older brother it was my job to protect him. But selfishly I'd shut myself off from everyone and in turn left Anthony to his own fate. His death left a huge void in my life. I became angry at the world and wanted revenge. I wanted someone to suffer. I wanted to avenge my brother's death.

Once again, I lashed out at the world. Although I'd never taken drugs, I knew where to find them. I walked along Gloucester Road in Bristol, looking for a pusher. It didn't take me long before I found a guy in his twenties standing in the shadows a few steps away from the streetlight.

'How many?' he grunted as soon as he saw me approach.

I glanced down at his hands and spotted a wad of heroin wraps in his hands. I wanted to hurt him because he was selling something that had killed my brother. I walked over to him, grabbed his collar and bundled him into an alleyway. My head crunched against his skull as I head butted and kicked him to the floor. He was a skinny bloke and he crumpled onto the ground without much resistance. As I looked around, something occurred to me.

What if he had a knife or back up?

Thankfully, he had neither. I snatched the heroin from his hands and ran over to a street drain at the side of the kerb. I stared down at the dark and murky water below the grid.

'Watch this, you bastard,' I screamed as I threw each and every wrap down into their watery grave.

I thought I'd feel elated but as I glanced back at the pusher lying bloodied and battered on the floor, I knew that I'd failed. For every drug dealer like him operating in backstreet towns there were hundreds further up the chain keeping the industry going – I'd never be able to stop them all. Anthony's death wouldn't be the first or last – there was nothing I could do to stop the tide.

My brother's death did have one positive impact: I picked up the phone and called Clair. This time we spoke and cried together. Anthony's death had broken us all but it had also brought me back to my family.

With a second funeral to face in just over a year I hardly knew how we would get through it. In the end it turned out to be one of the bleakest days of my life. It never feels right burying a young person, but when that person is a member of your own family, the loss and pain you feel is indescribable.

In the end, I took James with me. I wanted to cry but I couldn't, not in front of my son. We took our seats at the back of the church and minutes later the coffin came in. A lump of emotion lodged so high in the back of my throat that I thought I'd choke on it. I glanced up as Anthony's coffin passed and I was so lost in my own grief that at first I didn't recognise the devastated old man trailing behind it. He was stooped and bent over so low that he looked as if someone had punched him clean in the stomach. It was my father but he was old and broken. My heart went out to him.

That man has lost his son and his wife, I thought.

This wasn't about me or what had gone before, only the here and now mattered and my dad looked absolutely destroyed. I wanted to reach out to him, to try and console him and take his pain away. I glanced down at James sitting beside me and wondered how I'd feel. How would I cope with such a loss? For the first time ever, my father looked vulnerable. He'd lost his wife and now Anthony, the apple of his eye. After the church service we filed out and travelled to the crematorium. I kept my eye out for Dad and as soon as I could, I walked over to speak to him.

'How are you?' I began.

Dad looked up at me but he was so broken that no amount of words could ever hope to help or heal him. I looked away. It felt awkward and uncomfortable standing together but I refused to walk away because I needed him to know I was there for him.

'You alright?' he finally replied, breaking the silence.

It was far from a loving embrace but it was a chink of light and enough to thaw the ice that had frozen between us so many years before.

Afterwards, the wake was crowded with too many people drinking. Even though we'd just laid Anthony to rest, the mood was light as people reminisced about their time spent with him. As I glanced across the room I realised how uncomfortable Dad was. Suddenly, he stood up and headed over towards the door and left. I followed him.

Dad had left the front door ajar so I followed him inside. As I walked into the front room there he was, sitting in a chair staring off into the middle distance. I wanted to put my arm around him but didn't know how.

'Dad,' I said, not daring to look at him. 'We're gonna be alright from now on, aren't we?'

I held my breath as I waited for an answer.

'Yes.'

I almost wept with relief because right now I realised that I needed my family more than ever. We talked some more and I realised what I'd been missing. As the clock ticked by I finally felt ready to ask him.

'What was all that about when I was a kid then?'

The words were awkward because I was still haunted by what had happened with Mum, but the child inside me still needed to know. I needed answers and right now, sitting here, it felt okay to ask.

'What?' Dad replied at first looking up at me. His face was startled but he knew what I was talking about.

At first he refused to be drawn on the matter but I thought of Mum and Anthony, and I didn't know how long I had left with him. I needed an answer, so I pressed on. Finally, he took a deep breath and spoke.

'I was just trying to toughen you up,' he said.

I shook my head in despair: he'd done that alright. But at least now I had an answer. Afterwards, we talked some more and buried the hatchet.

But the months that followed weren't as easy to deal with. Two bereavements in such a short time hit me hard and I lost myself at the bottom of a bottle yet again. When I was offered another job in America, similar to the one I'd had in

London, I saw my chance. However, as soon as they checked out my application and saw my criminal record, they turned me down flat.

My brother's ashes were buried along with our mother's at a small church in Frampton Cotterell. One day I decided to visit, taking a friend of Anthony's with me. She'd been finding it hard to cope with his death too so I hoped a visit to the grave would bring her some closure. We stood there talking about Anthony when I noticed her face blanch white as if she'd seen a ghost. I turned to see my father standing right behind us. He was furious that I'd taken someone to the grave without his permission; a row ensued and within minutes I felt like a child again.

'Oh, fuck this,' I huffed as I walked away and out of the churchyard.

I knew I couldn't fall out with Dad forever because apart from my sisters, he was the only family I had left. If I walked away now I knew I'd never see him again, so I called Clair. She managed to smooth things over but, after that day, things were never the same again.

If I thought my life had hit an all-time low, losing Mum and then Anthony, I was wrong. Perhaps it was punishment for all my misdemeanours, who knows, but what I didn't realise then was that my life was about to change course in the blink of an eye.

CHAPTER TWELVE

Tears in the Darkness

THE VISION IN my right eye had been blurred for the best part of six years and had steadily worsened. My diabetes meant I still had to undergo regular eye check-ups at the hospital, which I always passed with flying colours. The hospital carried out the routine checks because I was told my diabetes carried a risk of blindness, even though with proper checks it was certainly rare. I presumed the annual checks would pick up any potential problems before they had chance to surface. My last check-up had been five months before and, apart from the blurring, which they'd put down to a bit of wear and tear, everything was fine.

'We'll just keep an eye on that,' the nurse replied without realising what she'd said.

I laughed at her inadvertent joke.

'Oops,' she giggled, putting a hand to her mouth.

But my jokes hid the fact that I was depressed and drinking

even more heavily than usual. To be honest, I didn't even care because I half expected to die any day. The drink had done this to me; it had depressed me. I was still tortured about Mum because in many ways I felt responsible for her death. The fact I'd asked her for answers the day before she died convinced me I was somehow to blame. Each day continued with the same pattern of self-loathing as the months passed by.

It was a cold day in February 2010, when my right eye felt even more blurred than normal. Some days were always worse than others and today was a bad day. Up until now, the blurring had mostly been in one corner but now it had spread right across my eye. Instead of dealing with it, I ignored it and convinced myself it had got worse because I'd been working long hours, plus all those years welding were bound to have had some effect. This time though there was something else. It was stinging.

I'd been at work all day and had managed to do my job but by the time I got home my right eye felt sore and tired. I instinctively rubbed it with the back of my hand but when I pulled my fingers away my sight wasn't any clearer, if anything, it was worse. I decided a good night's sleep would sort me out so I got undressed and climbed into bed. Even though my right eye was stinging, as soon as my head hit the pillow I fell fast asleep.

The following morning the alarm sounded so I stretched out a sleepy arm to try and switch it off. I needed to get up for work and, even though I knew what time it was I instinctively opened my eyes to check the clock. All I could see was nothingness. I rubbed my eyes and stared back at it again but nothing registered. Nothing. It was like being in a room with no window: everything was dark. I thought I might still be dreaming so I shook my head and blinked my eyes again to make sure they were fully open. As light tried to filter through I stared and stared but my sight felt strange and alien.

My left eye, which I'd never had any trouble with, had a big black blotch right in the middle of it. I blinked again but couldn't see a thing. My heart started to beat ten to the dozen with fear. My left eye had always been the better one but now it was as if someone had draped a big black bin liner over the middle of it. My breathing became shallow as panic set in.

Was I blind? No, I reasoned, trying to calm myself down.

Of course I wasn't blind; this was just a blip and something I'd have to sort out. I'd have to see a doctor, today. But in truth, I was starting to get really frightened. I held my hands out in front of my face and splayed my fingers in mid air but I couldn't see them. I squinted to see if I could make out any shapes but I couldn't, instead there was just a film of dark red blood. My hand was still shaking as I covered my right eye and stared hard through the left.

Maybe the right eye was causing the left one to overwork and go blind?

But there was nothing, just red with a black blob floating in the middle. I quickly switched hands and covered my left eye hoping it'd be better but it wasn't. My right eye, which had been blurred for some time, was now washed out and faded as though someone had drawn the world against a grey piece of paper and rubbed it all out again. I could just about decipher the faint outlines of large objects but that was it. The emptiness terrified me, a world with no colour or shapes, a deserted world. My worst fear as a diabetic had come true – I'd gone blind overnight. With my eyesight failing with every second, I knew I had to do something.

I staggered to my feet and automatically held my arms out to steady myself. I bent down and stretched out a hand to feel around for my jeans. As soon as the fabric brushed against my fingers I was grateful that I'd thrown them on top of the bed the night before. I pulled on a jumper. I couldn't tell if it was the right way round or not but I didn't care. My breathing became laboured as I tried to think straight.

Using small shuffling steps I tried to manoeuvre myself from the bedroom towards the front door but hit my leg against something sharp. I put a hand down to rub my shin and felt a sharp corner – I'd just hit the coffee table.

My heart beat like a wild animal whilst my other senses heightened. I knew I had to get out of the flat and call for help. I tried to picture in my mind where I was and how to get to the front door. I stumbled over something else – shoes – I'd left them on the floor the night before.

'Shit!' I cursed as my body fell forward and slammed against the wall.

I dipped down and felt around for them before slipping them on. I took each step as if I was walking out into the unknown, which in many ways, I was. A few more steps and I'd be at the front door. I ran my fingers along the wall and they bumped along the surface as I located the light switch. Almost there.

My shoes scuffed against the carpet in the communal hallway. Just a few more steps...

My mind whirred as I held out my arms and reached for signs that I'd made it. Something sharp caught against my third finger, a curved metal edge, the lip of the chain latch, which was thankfully undone. My fingers fumbled against the oval shaped door lock. I twisted it and immediately felt the cold morning breeze brush against my face. I was outside.

I tried to picture the pathway leading to the street. Were there any obstacles? I couldn't remember. What if I tripped and landed against the concrete smashing my head on the ground, what then? I'd be easy prey for any passing mugger.

I pushed down my arms in front of me. If I was blind, I sure as hell wasn't going to look it. My senses remained on full alert as I listened out for footsteps of anyone passing. I waited for what seemed like an eternity. Suddenly, in the distance I heard the tell-tale clacking of heels against pavement. Someone was coming and, from the noise, it sounded like a woman. Relief flooded through me.

Click, clack, click, clack, they went as the footsteps came closer.

'Help!' I called out into the distance. I tried to visualise the woman and where she was.

'Can you call me a cab?' I called again, my voice loud and urgent.

She sensed my distress and came over to help.

'It's my eyes,' I said pointing at them, 'I can't see.'

'Do you need an ambulance?' the woman asked, a little shocked.

I shook my head, this was central London, and God only knows how long an ambulance would take. I needed a cab and I needed one now. I heard her unclip something with her hand. Her bag, I hoped. I prayed she was taking out her mobile phone to call someone. Thankfully she was because then I heard her voice.

'Yes, that's right,' she was saying, confirming the address. 'It's urgent, how long will it be?'

The phone bleeped as she ended the call.

'There's a cab on its way,' she said patting my arm sympathetically but her voice sounded a little wary as if she really wasn't sure what to do next. I was a random stranger and I could tell she didn't really want to get involved.

'It's okay,' I reassured her. 'I'll be fine. And thanks, thanks for calling me a cab.'

Although my voice was calm, inside I was shaking.

The woman turned and walked away and suddenly I felt very alone again. I wanted her to turn back, to stay with me and hold my hand but I knew I'd done this. I'd done it to myself and now I'd have to try and fix it.

A few minutes later, I heard the sound of tyres against tarmac as the cab pulled up. The taxi driver got out to help me. I tried to take control of myself and stay calm. I could just about see the faded outline of his car so when he opened the door, I climbed inside.

'Where to, mate?' he asked as I heard him slump back down in the driver's seat.

'I'm having a bit of trouble seeing. Can you take me to Moorfields Eye Hospital?' I said as if it was an everyday occurrence; as if I went blind every single day of my life.

My survival instinct kicked in and I tried to act cool but inside I was falling apart. My stomach churned like a washing machine because I knew what this meant. I knew because I'd been warned about it and it had always been there at the back of my mind. My diabetes had hung over me like a black cloud throughout my life and now it was pissing down all over on me. I had never treated it with respect and now it was getting its own back. Now I was blind. I wanted to cry but what was the point? Crying wouldn't undo the damage.

It was 9am by the time the cab pulled up outside Moorfields Eye Hospital. The driver knew I needed assistance so he found me a nurse to help. I pulled out a note and handed it over, not bothering with the change. It could have been £10 or £20, but I didn't care, money didn't matter anymore.

My hands were still trembling as the nurse led me off to a room somewhere. My sight was still blurred but I could just about make her out through the haze. I felt safe, she'd know what to do, she'd help me.

'I can't see,' I said my voice rising with panic. 'I could see last night although not very well. My right eye was blurred and stinging but now my left eye has gone too. All I can see is a big black blotch and it's freaking me out,' I garbled.

The nurse ran off to fetch a consultant who shone something into my eyes. I only knew what he was doing because he told me. The fact I couldn't see it absolutely petrified me.

'Help me,' I begged. 'I'm so scared.'

The consultant seemed to take an age but when he spoke his voice was grave with concern.

'We need to get you into theatre as soon as possible Mr Tovey... are you diabetic?'

'Yes,' I answered. 'I am. They always said something like this could happen. Is this it then, am I blind?' Fear choked the words at the back of my throat. Blind. I was just 42 years old.

'We need to get you into theatre right now,' the doctor explained before speaking to the nurse. 'We'll need him to sign some consent forms.'

'What do you think it is doctor?' I said, interrupting. 'Am I blind? Will my eyes get better?'

The consultant cleared his throat as if buying extra time. He chose his words carefully and, although I was listening, nothing was really sinking in.

'If it is what I suspect it is then you have what we call late-stage aggressive diabetic retinopathy. It means we need to get you into surgery as soon as possible to prevent any further damage.'

He explained the blurring in my right eye was possibly glaucoma but he said he'd know more once he'd got me into theatre. I think he already knew it was too late to save my sight but he didn't want to commit until he was absolutely certain.

As a long-term diabetic, I'd always known my eyesight was at risk. High blood sugar levels can cause damage to the back of the eye – the retina. I'd always presumed my yearly checks would pick up any problems but this had happened so quickly – in the blink of an eye – that they didn't have a chance. I'd simply gone to bed sighted and woken up blind.

I was unable to see the clock on the hospital ward so I don't know how long I waited, but I seemed to be wheeled down to surgery very quickly. Once there, I underwent a two-hour laser eye operation yet, despite my surgeon's best attempts, it was too late to save my sight. When I finally came around I was in complete darkness. Everything was black and empty but I guessed I was lying in a hospital bed. The eye patches taped across my face felt hot and itchy and I was frightened. I was so used to having control of my life but now it had disappeared overnight. I felt scared, as if someone had turned the light out in my life.

Up until this moment I hadn't realised how much I

depended on my eyes. Like everyone else, I'd taken them for granted. But now all I had was my hearing, my sense of smell and my touch to guide me. I listened carefully as I tried to jigsaw my environment together along with who was in it. Suddenly someone swept past my bed and a slight draft blew against the skin of my arm.

'Nurse?' I called out to a blackened world.

'Hello,' a voice replied. 'How are you feeling John?'

I wanted to shout out *I'm effing blind, how do you think I'm feeling?* but the words wouldn't come, my voice had been stolen by the shock of it all.

'I... I...' I mumbled, still a little groggy from the anaesthetic.

'It's okay John, I'll go and fetch the doctor who will speak to you. Now, have you got anyone you'd like me to call?' she asked.

But I didn't, I wanted to deal with this myself. A few moments later, a weight landed on my bed as someone perched on the side of it.

'How are you feeling?' a voice asked. It was the doctor.

'Am I blind?' I asked immediately. 'Will I ever be able to see again?' The words jarred in my throat making them all too real.

'You have what we call advanced retinopathy. It was quite an aggressive form but we did everything we could; we tried our very best.'

My mind whirred, what did he mean? I was desperate to read his eyes, to see his face, to try and work out just what he meant but all those things I once took for granted had gone. Instead, I listened for clues in his voice, which sounded downbeat and defeatist.

'So are you saying I'm blind?' I asked bluntly.

'We're not sure. It'll take a day or so for your eyes to settle down. Only then will we know if the operation has been a success or not.'

After he left, I pulled away the tape from the edge of each eye patch: I had to know now. As I peeled away the left patch, I opened my eye and could see a very faded outline. It was like looking through dirty water. Smaller black blotches floated around indiscriminately. I taped it back up again in case the light damaged it. I held my breath as I uncovered the right. It was still faded, like an old photograph bleached to nothing, just grey and colourless. This was as good as it was going to get, I just had a gut-feeling. This was my life now.

The following day both eye patches were removed for good. I prayed for light but instead my world revealed itself as a milky grey darkness. My hands began to tremble; I was blind.

It took me a few days to realise that this was it. To be honest, I think the op had been a complete waste of time. Part of me wondered what would have happened if I'd gone to the hospital the night before; would it have made any difference? I shook the thought from my head. There was little point torturing myself with the what-ifs and what-might-have-beens. Instead I signed myself out. They offered me follow-up appointments but I didn't want anything more to do with them. I needed to get back to Bristol, I needed to go home.

I contacted a friend who picked me up and took me back home by train. I was bitter, angry and still in denial. I bought a drink on the train and one followed another. I was so drunk that my blood sugar rocketed because I hadn't bothered to take my medication: what was the point? The worst had already happened. By the time the train arrived in Bristol, I was in such a bad way that I was rushed to Frenchay Hospital, where doctors put me on drip.

'What's the point?' I told the nurse, my voice full of self-pity. 'I may as well be dead.'

I stayed in hospital for four or five days until doctors managed to get my blood sugar levels under control. During this time I was visited by the hospital social worker who arranged emergency accommodation for me because the hospital had nowhere to discharge me to. I was placed in a bed and breakfast but, because of my disability, within a few weeks, I was moved again, this time to a flat.

Even though the area was passable, my new flat was surrounded by druggies. I'd lived in some rough places in London, but nothing compared to this. At least before I'd been able to escape because I was at work for 12–14 hours a day, but now I was stuck in my hell-hole and it became my prison. The communal stairway was disgusting and constantly stank of piss and cannabis. The flat was small and cramped inside but it didn't matter, I'd abandoned most of my possessions in London, sentimental things that could never be replaced.

My flat was a small one-bedroom apartment on the first floor of a high-rise block. It was so small that you couldn't fit a double bed inside – not that I'd ever need one of those again – now I was blind, no woman would ever want me.

I hated my new home but I hated leaving it even more because I felt so vulnerable. I missed vital appointments at the eye hospital in Bristol. My condition needed to be regularly monitored but I refused. I was offered lots of help but I stuck my fingers up to them all because I didn't want anyone's help or pity. In many ways it felt kind of stupid, like locking the door after the horse had bolted. I just wanted to be left alone to crawl into a hole and die.

One evening, I was sat alone inside my flat. Sirens blared away from the street outside, dogs barked and people shouted. It was as though I'd been transported right back to my childhood but instead of a house of angry people, I lived in a neighbourhood full of it.

A few weeks after I moved in, a letter popped through my door. Unable to read it, I asked the bloke downstairs to tell me what it said. He was usually a pleasant guy but this time he seemed reluctant to help.

'I just need to know what it says,' I said getting a little shirty.

'It's from the council, John,' he began.

'What do they want?' I snapped.

I heard paper rustle in his hands as he began to read.

'It's about you playing your Madness records too loud.'

'What?'

There was a silence and then my neighbour spoke.

'Erm, it was me. I reported you.'

'Why?' I demanded, a little perturbed.

'Because I thought you were dead John,' he explained. 'I rang the police so that someone would go and check on you. I never see you and I was worried. But instead of the police, it looks as if they got the council involved.'

My mind raced back to the week before. An odd thing had happened and, at the time it had made no sense whatsoever. I started to giggle until soon I was laughing away like a madman.

'What?' the neighbour asked. 'What's so funny?'

'The police did knock the other week and, when I didn't answer, they kicked my bloody door in. At 7.30 in the morning!'

I sighed as I recalled how they'd given me a right fright. The neighbour had been right, my Madness CD had been on full blast when they burst into my bedroom. My first thought was *bloody hell, they've found me. What have I done?*

'Sorry John,' my neighbour apologised. 'I just needed to know you were okay. I haven't seen you because you keep yourself locked up all day in that flat of yours.'

'It's okay,' I replied, and it was. It was nice to know that someone cared.

The funniest part for me was that the council had actually named the band in the wording of the 'nuisance' letter. I thought how much it would make them laugh. Environmental Health had been right about my music though: I played it constantly. Anything to stop me from sleeping, because when I fell asleep, I dreamed I could see.

I'd go to bed drunk and 'see' my son James, calling out to me. On other occasions I would dream I was back at work doing my job and loving every minute of it but, inevitably, I'd wake up and realise it was all in my imagination. I was blind and I'd never see again.

I'd have nightmares too. I'd be back on the train with the gang: trapped and surrounded, or stuck inside the boys' unit. I'd have fights on a massive scale and ones I could never hope to win. My mind had exploded, going off in all different directions.

I drank so much that I would wake up face down in pools of my own vomit. I tried to wash away my troubles before using alcohol but now I was drinking myself into oblivion, just to forget I was blind. At least when I was asleep I could see. Whether it was a dream or a nightmare, at least I was fully-sighted. The stark reality was I'd always have to wake up the following morning and face my blindness all over again. The drinking coupled with my diabetes was a sure-fire way to an early grave but instead of stopping I just drank more and more, hoping that I'd never wake up again.

One day, I came around on the floor of my bedroom.

I'm still here, a voice screamed inside my head.

I was so desperate that I wanted to kill myself but as my hands searched for tablets, I realised that I was far too much of a coward to go through with it. I was a broken man who'd lost everything. Maybe this was my punishment for leading such a terrible life, maybe it was all I deserved?

I played my Madness *Rise and Fall* album on repeat although, since the letter, I turned the volume down. Their music had kept me going through some of the darkest moments of my life but even Madness couldn't give me my sight back. I thought back to my days as a skinhead on Minehead seafront. If I concentrated hard enough I could picture it so clearly that I could almost taste the salt in the breeze and smell the fish and chips cooking along the promenade. But that's all I had now; memories.

My mobile phone buzzed constantly but most of the time I ignored it whilst with others I was far too drunk to answer. Unbeknown to me, my ex-wife Tracey was frantic with worry and trying to contact me. So was James, my sister and my friends but I ignored them all. My confidence had been shattered into a thousand different pieces and I didn't have a clue how to fix myself. If friends called at the front door buzzing the intercom, I'd tell them to fuck off.

'I don't want your pity,' I'd scream before hanging up.

One day the intercom buzzed so I dished out my usual volley of abuse.

'Er, I'm from TV licensing,' a shocked voice replied.

I burst out laughing.

'Well, you can eff off as well because I don't even own a bleeding TV and even if I did, I couldn't watch it because I'm blind!'

There was an audible gasp over the other end of the intercom.

'Well,' came the reply. 'I still need to check because on our records…'

I cut him off mid-sentence.

'Why don't you just fuck off and get a proper job?'

The man scarpered and didn't knock again. I thought how ironic it was I didn't have a TV, not because I was blind, but because I always hated it. The TV had ruled our house as a child so my hatred had grown over many years. Still, shouting at the TV licensing man had been wrong: it wasn't his fault I was blind. I'd turned into a monster.

When I'd lost my sight it was as though I'd lost my identity. I missed seeing my face in the mirror every morning. I was worried I'd forget what I looked like – maybe I'd even forget who I was? It didn't seem that far-fetched because I was slowly losing myself piece by piece. I didn't want anyone to see me like this because I could only begin to imagine what I'd become.

As usual, I found solace in booze but getting hold of it was a different matter. I was alone and vulnerable so I'd wait until later in the day when there were fewer people around; only then I'd venture out. I'd scurry along pavements to the local off-licence to buy whatever alcohol I could. I'd spend all my money on strong cider, whisky or vodka – a potent cocktail. It blackened my heart and soul and made them as dark as my world.

My system was easy. I made mental notes as I worked my way along the path towards the shop using my outstretched arms to guide me. Surgery hadn't worked but I still had some blurred 'vision', enough to make out people or objects. I'd feel my way along walls and hedges, staggering and a little unstable on my feet, like a bloke who'd had too much to drink. I tried hard to look as if I was fully-sighted. I knew that if I looked blind then I'd become a prime target to mug or beat up. With no visual aids other than my remaining senses I was on constant full-alert, ready to attack or defend myself at a moment's notice. If someone approached, my heartbeat would quicken and I'd listen out for their footsteps to make sure they'd walked away and weren't coming back to attack me.

I convinced myself my disability was karma for all the bad things I'd done in life, that my past had come back to haunt me and make me as vulnerable as one of my victims.

Convinced my blindness was my own fault, I sank into an even deeper depression until soon my daily diet consisted of just chips and booze. I didn't have the guts to kill myself so I decided I'd drink myself to death instead. My unhealthy lifestyle made me pile on the weight. I'd always been a slim Jim, around 13 stone, but now I'd ballooned to over 16 stone. I was injecting myself with insulin because I didn't want to have hypos but I suffered with constant hangovers and felt so dreadful that even getting out of bed was a struggle. Now I was blind and fat!

After seven months, the phone rang less and less. Everyone had given up on me and I was glad because I didn't want their pity. However one day when my mobile phone rang something made me answer. I couldn't see the name flashing up on the screen so I took a chance and picked it up, getting ready to shout abuse down the line. I'd already drunk myself halfway down a whisky bottle when I heard a familiar voice on the other end of the line: it was Pippa, Tracey's eldest daughter.

'Hello, John John,' she said in a voice as soft and as gentle as I remembered. 'John John' was Pippa's nickname for me.

The blackness momentarily lifted from my heart and, for the first time in months, I remembered who I was. Children don't care if you're blind. They don't see the bigger picture: they love you, warts and all.

'Hello,' I whispered slowly, my voice cracking with emotion. I was drunk and conscious of it but I didn't want my slurred speech to frighten her.

'How are you John John? I haven't seen you for a while. When will I see you again?' Pippa asked.

My heart thudded inside my chest and I felt sick with guilt. I'd abandoned everyone, even my two nieces.

'Soon,' I replied choking back my tears.

'Promise?'

'Promise. I'll come and see you very soon.' I replied and with that I hung up.

I felt disgusted that I'd answered the phone to a child, drunk. As soon as the call ended I buried my face in my hands and sobbed my heart out. I cried and cried until I had no more tears left, or so I thought. I walked over to the sink and turned the cold tap on full. I filled up the bowl with ice-cold water and splashed my face. The tears had stopped but the guilt and self-loathing were still there. Soon, I'd started to sob again. I cried until I was emotionally spent. If I hadn't hit rock bottom before, I had now. As I sobered up I cringed. I knew I couldn't go on like this. I needed to give myself an almighty kick up the arse, stop feeling sorry for myself and get help.

I thought I'd lost everything but I hadn't, because I had two little girls who loved and needed me and of course James, my amazing son. He deserved better and so did all my friends and family. It was time to start again.

As the fog of inebriation lifted, I saw things more clearly for the first time in ages. I thought back to all those I'd lost: Mum, my brother, Shaun and Lee. Sure my life was different now but at least I still had a life; at least I was still alive. I needed to pick myself up, dust myself off and get back out there and face the world. It was time for my comeback and now I was ready.

CHAPTER THIRTEEN

First Steps

'HELLO,' I BEGAN, my voice strained and a little nervous. I swallowed hard so I could get the next words out without faltering.

'My name is John Tovey and I'm blind.'

There, I'd said it. I said the one word I'd avoided using for the past seven months. The one word that, if uttered, would make it all too real. But this was real and now I needed professional help.

I was standing in Bristol Eye Hospital, speaking to a lady from the RNIB. She looked up my records but she didn't need to, I knew what it said: non-attendance for almost every single appointment.

A friend had taken me that morning, helping me to make the journey by bus. In the end, I had to catch two and it had been both noisy and frightening not being able to see my way through the crowds in the city centre.

I faced the lady and continued. 'I know I've missed loads of appointments but I'm here now. I know I need some professional help if I'm going to start accepting what's happened.'

I felt ashamed and embarrassed. I'd been offered lots of help but I'd refused it all. I'd tried to cope alone but I'd failed miserably. The woman listened patiently as I explained how isolated I felt.

'Have you got a cane?' she asked.

I was puzzled.

'You mean a white stick?' I replied, slightly appalled.

'Yes.'

'Er, no, I haven't.'

I didn't want to carry a white cane. If I did then everyone would know I was blind and how defenceless I really was.

'I think it would help,' the woman continued.

I wanted to protest but I knew that if I was going to accept things I had to start taking advice from the people who knew best. So, when she handed me a single white cane I took it. The cane felt odd in my hand, hard and abrupt, like a flashing neon sign to the rest of the world.

The RNIB lady was patient. She made me an appointment for the following day at RNIB headquarters where I would meet with a counsellor called Adam.

'In order to accept it, you need to be able to talk about it,' she explained.

I took the appointment and, with the cane in my hand, made my way along the corridor towards the exit with my friend. I felt ashamed of the cane and part of me wanted to throw it in the bin. Even though I couldn't see, I felt as if every passing person was looking at me but I'd given up before and I was determined not to now.

Instead of hiding the cane when I got on the bus, I held it in my hand and, when no one bumped into me, it was a revelation. Even when I accidently knocked into someone, they didn't say a word. I didn't have to either because the cane explained everything. That day I returned home with mixed emotions. I was all churned up inside, unsure if I was doing the right thing. I wondered what a do-good counsellor could tell me about my life, and how the hell would this Adam even know how I felt?

The following day I awoke and travelled to the RNIB headquarters in Bedminster.

'I'm not mad,' I told Adam as soon as I walked into the room.

I couldn't see him but I hated the idea of a stranger judging me. But I soon found out Adam didn't judge, he listened. Before I knew it, a whole hour had passed by. I was worried what I'd talk about but as soon as the floodgates opened all my thoughts and fears came spilling out. It wasn't until the end of the session that Adam dropped a bombshell of his own.

'John, I'm blind too,' he told me in a matter-of-fact voice.

I was completely gobsmacked. How could he be blind, he sounded too bloody upbeat and positive!

'Really?' I asked. 'What happened to you?'

Adam explained how he'd lost his sight at the age of 25. I listened in stunned silence as he told me how he'd never let a little thing like blindness hold him back.

'I still go out to the pub with my mates,' he chirped.

'Do you?' I gasped shaking my head in disbelief.

'Yeah, I still get chatted up by women and I've had a few girlfriends along the way,' he chuckled.

It made me smile.

'I thought my life was over as far as women were concerned,' I admitted.

'No, not at all,' Adam explained.

By the end of the session I felt like a totally different person and as if a huge weight had been lifted off my shoulders. I'd gone into that room with my chin on the floor, wrapped up in my own self-pity but I left feeling so much more positive.

Before I arrived, I'd wondered how Adam could ever understand what I was going through but I was wrong. He'd been there, done it and bought the T-shirt, only at a much younger age. I'd have never have guessed such a happy and remarkable young man was blind, just like me.

If he can cope with it then so can I, I told myself.

It was the start of a long journey but I had taken the first steps on my road to recovery.

Soon I was looking forward to my next counselling session. In fact, I didn't see it as a counselling session but more like a chat with someone who knew what it felt like to be me. For the first time in ages, I was able to think things through more clearly. Adam was such a positive influence in my life that soon I started 'seeing' the bigger picture. He'd been blind for years but he didn't let a little thing like losing his sight get in the way. He became my inspiration. All the bits of life I missed such as going out to the pub, talking to women and making new friends, he was still enjoying.

'I never thought I'd do those things again,' I said shaking my head.

'Of course you will!' Adam explained. 'John, life doesn't stop just because you're blind.'

Slowly, my sense of humour started chipping its way back to the surface.

'At least the next time I'm out with mates I won't be first to the bar, so I suppose I'll save a bit of money,' I joked. Adam laughed and I did too. It felt good.

With each session I opened up more and more. Adam was my lifesaver and soon I'd finished my ten counselling sessions. For the first time in ages I stopped feeling sorry for myself and started looking at all the positives in my life. Sure, I didn't have my eyes to guide me but at least I could walk and talk. I could still listen to my beloved Madness: imagine if I'd lost my hearing too? I shuddered at the thought.

The more I thought about it, the more I had to be grateful for. I still had my smell and touch senses, and I was surrounded by some amazing people. I was blessed with a loving son, good friends and family. I realised I couldn't turn my back on them. All that time I'd been grieving for my old life but now it had gone and now it was time to move on. This was my life and it was for living.

I started to make contact with all those I'd shunned and, instead of pitying me as I'd first feared, everyone tried their best to help. James transferred my Madness records onto an MP3 player so I could listen to them at the push of a button. It meant the world to me and fast became my prized possession. I stopped grieving for the old John, and started being thankful for what I had. I realised that far from being doomed I was, in fact, a very fortunate man.

It was hard but I also started to get my drinking under control. I accepted my situation and slowly, as the fog lifted, I began to function as a human being once more. As an added bonus once I cut back on alcohol, my remaining senses sharpened even more.

Three months into my period of rehabilitation, I started carrying a long mobility cane with me all the time. It was a longer cane rather than the short 'symbol' cane the RNIB had given me. I knew the stick marked me out from others, like wearing a badge telling everyone I was blind, but now I was useless without it. I used it to find my way along the pavement. As my confidence grew, the faster I walked as I tapped it against the floor. I must have looked like a right idiot walking along but no one said a word. If I'd expected abuse then I was wrong. If anything everyone did their best to help. It restored my faith in human nature.

Thanks to my RNIB mobility instructor, I was put on a list for a guide dog. I'd thought about having a guide dog ever since Adam had mentioned it in one of our counselling sessions although I questioned my ability to look after both a dog and myself. Also, I'd been warned it could be a long process and one I believed would never happen. Besides, I hardly deserved a dog like that given the life I'd had. Anyway, I needed to learn how to use a long cane first so I began my proper training.

Two ladies came out to my flat to help me adapt to my living environment. They gave me some basic equipment such as a talking clock that spoke the time and a key ring which was supposed to do the same but it was rubbish and constantly beeped instead. In the end, I became so frustrated that I smashed it up in a temper! They also gave me a cassette player and some audio books so that I could still enjoy 'reading', and a pair of dark glasses. I was grateful for the glasses because I was conscious of people looking at me, particularly my eyes, as there was nothing I could do to stop them darting around.

The training was much harder than I had expected. It was odd taking a step into the unknown and to begin with I was a little apprehensive but I realised it was the only way forward. The long cane was altogether different from the short one I had become used to. I learned to tap it in order to get a feel of where I was. With the help of Clara, my mobility instructor, I learned to feel for kerb edges and obstacles. As I slowly got to grips with my new way of life I was amazed at how good it made me feel.

'I should've done this months ago,' I admitted.

With each day I started to feel a little better about my situation. In short, that simple stick gave me my life back. As I tapped my way successfully along roads and pavements, a smile returned to my face once more. I was starring in my own special version of 'One Step Beyond', only not quite how Madness would have pictured it!

As my confidence soared so did my personal happiness and, for the first time in ages, I accepted help from strangers. The last time I'd accepted 'help', I was locked up in a kids unit with perverts but now I trusted and believed in others and it enabled me to live again.

With a new lust for life, I contacted some old friends, Kevin and Liza and another couple called Bob and Katherine. They were amazing and didn't judge or pity me. Instead they took me under their wing and kept me busy until soon I was out socialising again. They'd take me to the pub or on short weekend breaks with their families. In short, they went out of their way to help me get back on my feet. I couldn't have wished or asked for better friends.

I started telling jokes and once I'd started there was no stopping me. I'd always loved to mess around but now I enjoyed being the class clown. It was a long process and in many ways it's one that is still on-going, but finally I started to accept my new life.

It had been Adam who had first mentioned having a guide dog and initially, I'd scoffed at the idea.

'Don't be silly,' I joked. 'I can't even look after myself, how would I be able to look after a dog?'

However the seed had been planted inside my head and from that moment on I couldn't stop thinking about it. I'd always loved animals because unlike people, animals didn't let you down. Animals, particularly dogs, offer an unconditional love that means that even if you mess up, you know you can always make things right again.

A few weeks later, Clara came to visit me. I asked her if she thought I was a suitable candidate for a dog. Clara said whilst I was, my flat certainly wasn't. So, in February 2011, after a year living in my hellhole, I moved to a new flat in a lovely village called Almondsbury, situated in an affluent area of Bristol. My new flat was much bigger than the old place but I soon mastered my way around.

I wrongly presumed that just because I'd moved, I'd get my dog pretty quickly but it didn't work like that and for good reason. I remained on the waiting list and in the meantime I started to lose weight and clean up my act. I was still living day by day but by now my drinking was under control. I still enjoyed the odd pint of beer but now I could take it or leave it. The answer to my problems didn't lie at the bottom of a whisky bottle and I knew from experience it certainly didn't make me feel any better. Before I'd used alcohol to try and escape from my problems but now I accepted them. In many ways, I felt as if I'd been reborn.

My life had changed in more ways than one. In my new home, instead of feeling vulnerable I immediately felt safe. I started going to the village shop – a community venture run by volunteers. It was only a short distance away but it was a lifeline for me. Also, it didn't sell cigarettes or booze, which was fantastic as all temptations were immediately removed from my life.

For the first time in years, I felt as if I could breathe again because I wasn't constantly on edge waiting for someone to attack me. It was a lovely neighbourhood that housed respectable families. I'd well and truly landed on my feet. It sounds over-dramatic but that little village and its residents gave me my life back. People accepted me for who I was and welcomed me with open arms. I was worried they'd find out about my chequered past so I decided to be honest and open with everyone who asked. If I worried it would drive the good people of Almondsbury away from me, I was wrong. They didn't judge or ostracise me, instead they vowed to help.

Three months later, a wonderful lady from Guide Dogs came to see me; her name was Emma Yard. Emma had the patience of a saint and organised for me to start training with a real-life guide dog. I was bursting with excitement and couldn't wait to start. A short while later Emma brought a guide dog called Volley, and together we went for a trial walk outside. I placed my hand on the metal brace attached to the dog and I tried my best not to grip too hard despite my nerves.

'Just try and relax your arm so that your thumb rests against the side of your leg.' Emma explained.

I did as she said but as soon as Volley started to walk, even with Emma at my side, I felt my arm fly straight out in front of me.

'No, John,' she said patiently.

We stopped so I could try it again but the same thing happened.

'I'm sorry,' I said apologising, 'but it feels as though he's running off.'

'He's just walking at a normal pace,' Emma told me.

What I was feeling was completely normal, she explained. It was my own natural fear holding me back. I tried to relax and off we set again only this time I felt as if I was being dragged along by an out of control lawn mower!

'Whoops!' I giggled, feeling a little daft as I cursed myself for not being able to get the hang of it.

'Don't worry,' Emma encouraged. 'It takes time and lots of practice.'

And it did. On a few occasions I felt like packing it all in and going back to my long cane but I wasn't a quitter now, I wanted to succeed. On the bad days my instincts mocked me and told me to crawl back into the bottle. Giving up would be easier than this, but I held my resolve. This was a daily fight but it was one I needed to win. I'd never been good at anything in my life; so far I'd managed to mess up everything but now I was desperate to learn and do well. I became the epitome of a swot, determined to come top of the class. If I was going to be blind then I was going to be bloody good at it!

But with all the practice in the world it still felt alien because I was putting all my trust in one animal. What I didn't realise is just how smart these amazing creatures are. Unlike me, Volley had trained hard for two years and knew his stuff. So did my next practice dog, Morris. These dogs were professionals; I was the amateur. I half expected to bump into stuff, to stumble or fall but I never did. Under Emma's expert guidance, something clicked and I found the more trust I put in the dogs, the quicker I learned.

One day I was walking around the village with who I thought was Volley. The walk had gone better than ever and by the time we'd finished I felt completely elated. But Emma had a confession.

'John, you know I said I had a dog in mind for you?'

I nodded my head.

'Well,' she said, 'This is your dog John, this is him. This is a dog called Dez and I think he's the dog for you.'

I gasped and knelt down against the beautiful creature at my side. Stretching out a hand, I ran my fingers along his back. Dez's fur felt soft and silken beneath my palm – it was love at first touch. I snuggled in close trying to get a cuddle off him and felt his furry face against my chin. A wet gravelly tongue licked my ear and felt so ticklish that it made me laugh out loud.

'Whoa there fella,' I chuckled. A grin spread across my face and I couldn't wipe it off because that day I fell in love.

Just like my beloved Madness, Dez gave off an aura of fun and love and quite literally bounced with happiness. When Emma took him home, I pined for my new mate. I just longed to be with him. But Emma explained it would take a week to sort out the paperwork before Dez became officially mine. As I waited for his arrival I felt excited and appre-hensive at the same time. Would I really be able to look after such a beautiful animal if so, how would I clean up after him? But Emma told me not to worry.

'You two will be just fine John,' she insisted.

I owed Emma so much. All the people I'd come into contact with had been brilliant but Emma was a cut above the rest. She didn't just teach me how to walk down the road with a dog; she prepared me psychologically so that I was in the right place to have Dez. I had asked Emma what he looked like and when she told me he was a beautiful black Labrador with big brown eyes, I held that image in my mind.

She smiled as she explained: 'He keeps looking up at you John, as if he's in love with you.'

The feeling was mutual.

'Or maybe he's just wondering how many biscuits I've got in my pocket?' I joked.

Emma gave me a list of things I'd need. I didn't have to buy a thing because Guide Dogs provided everything. But I went out and bought them because I wanted to. I was excited because it was like shopping for a new baby with me the proud and expectant father. A neighbour took me to a large, out of town pet shop where I spent over £100 – my entire savings – but I didn't care because Dez was worth it. At one point, I didn't have any electricity for two days because I'd spent all my money on Dez but it didn't matter; I just listened to my battery-powered radio and waited for his arrival.

I'd bought him a bed and more toys than one dog could ever want or need. This was the start of the rest of my life and one I'd share with my new pal. Dez was going to be the fella who would give me my freedom back but more importantly, I knew we would be best friends for the rest of our lives.

CHAPTER FOURTEEN

My Boy

A S SOON AS Dez arrived we became inseparable. We were meant to spend the weekend together so that we could 'bond', but our special bond developed almost immediately.

Just like the Madness song. An earthquake had erupted, and that earthquake was Dez.

He bounded through my door, into my flat and stole my heart. There was no turning back; this big black gorgeous Labrador was here to stay!

The first morning I awoke to find Dez on top of my bed breathing into my face urging me to get the hell up and out of bed. He followed me around all that day. In fact, he was so eager to please that he almost turned into a bloody trip hazard!

'Hey, there you are boy,' I said stretching out a hand to check where he was. I gave his head a friendly pat and he lapped it up, gratefully nuzzling his head into my palm.

I heard the tell-tale tip tap of his paws against laminate floor as he padded over to fetch one of his toys.

'In a minute mate, I'm just going for a shower.' I felt guilty leaving him for even a second.

I automatically closed the bathroom door behind me. I'd lived on my own for years and always did the same thing. My hand felt along the windowsill until I located the square form of the radio. I ran a finger across the top and clicked it on. The reception crackled and fired into life. Someone was reading the headlines and, as I twisted on the shower, the water drowned out the sound blaring away in the background.

I stripped off my clothes and felt down for the edge of the bath, gingerly placing a foot inside. I had to be careful, the bath was slippery even with the mat, and I knew I couldn't afford to take a tumble, not with Dez to look after.

The radio continued to warble on in the background as I climbed into the shower. I pulled the thin plastic curtain across and allowed the water to wash all over me. A short while later, clean and refreshed, I turned off the shower and dragged my hands across my face and hair to rid myself of the excess water. I felt the edge of the bath again to steady myself. Climbing out was even more treacherous than getting in. I lifted up my right foot high in the air to clear the side of the bathtub and put my foot down on to the mat. But as soon as my toes hit it I felt something odd underfoot. It was warm, moving and made of fur.

'Dez!' I exclaimed.

I pulled my foot back up and tried hard not to lose my balance. I hadn't been expecting a bathroom mat with a heartbeat!

'Are you alright down there mate?' I asked stretching out a hand to feel for my new buddy.

I carefully crouched down inside the bath so that I could reach down and check on him. A wet tongue lashed out and kissed me against my arm.

'Hey, you, what are you doing there,' I chuckled, patting him on top of his big square head. 'You daft lump, I could've squashed you!'

Dez got to his feet and started to fuss around me. He pushed his nose right against my face and began to sniff.

'Nice and clean Dez.' I quipped. 'What do you think to my shower gel; do I smell nice?'

Soon I was laughing away to myself like a madman. I crouched inside the bath naked and blind trying to check on this daft dog who was so desperate to be with me that he'd sneaked in and hidden down on the floor at the side of the bath.

His head suddenly dropped away and I dipped a hand down to run it across his back to work out where he was. I smiled as I felt a curled up furry lump bunched up right against the bathtub. Within minutes it was snoring.

I was getting cold so I grabbed a towel off the rail and wrapped it around me. I wondered how Dez had got in and then I remembered the door, it had no lock. He'd been so keen to follow that he'd simply barged his way in. I hadn't heard the door swing open because of the radio.

'I guess I'm gonna have to watch my step with you around Dezzy boy,' I laughed.

I dipped a tentative toe out and against the bathroom floor and felt around to second-guess where he was. He was still asleep so I stepped across his slumbering body. Well, he as sure as hell wasn't going to be the one to move! As I dried myself, I heard him scurry back up onto his feet. After that, he followed me everywhere I went.

A short while later Dez was at the back door. I heard his tail swinging and tapping away on the laminate like an impatient foot. I opened it and Dez ran out for what I guessed was a call of nature.

'Busy, busy,' I cried after him.

The words were code for 'go to the toilet'. Emma had taught me it along with many others. There was so much to remember that I was worried I'd forget some of it. With no sight to guide me, I stuck my ear out of the door and listened for him. Right on cue I heard Dez weeing his heart out.

'Good boy,' I said as he brushed past. I could just imagine him shaking his head as if to say, *Blimey, it was only a wee!*

Fishing a hand inside my pocket, I pulled out a dog treat. Dez was soon there and had devoured it within seconds. I heard his nose against the floor as he sniffed around for any loose crumbs. But I was holding back on dog treats like a class leader holding back chocolate at a slimming club. Emma had warned how much weight Labs can put on. They're loving and loyal dogs who would give you the world but they're also very greedy. I was determined my Dez wouldn't become obese or ruined with kindness.

'No more,' I laughed as he sniffed desperately at my fingers.

Dez wanted more and now I could feel his nose sniffing up around the pocket of my jeans. I needed to use a distraction technique.

'Here,' I called throwing Dez's toy outside.

The toy squeaked as Dez picked it up in his mouth and ran back over towards me.

'You want me to throw it again?' I asked. I couldn't see him but I almost felt his eyes burning into me, begging me to chuck the toy again. I felt down and got a handful of whiskers and then the edge of the toy.

'Come on then,' I said taking it from his mouth. 'Go and fetch.'

I heard his claws scurry against the concrete as he ran off onto the grass. He was a bit slower but soon he was back with the toy pushing in into my hand. This was great! I threw it again.

'Go on Dez!'

But this time there was no noise, no scurrying. Nothing.

'Dez!' I shouted in a panic.

I put my arms right out in front of me to feel for him. I knew my back garden was safe and secure with six-foot high fences all around but I panicked. What if he'd escaped and run off? My heart was in my mouth. I spread out my fingers and felt into the empty distance and as I did, a wet nose bobbed against my open palm. I put my other hand against my chest to calm my pounding heart and sighed with relief.

'You're there!' I gasped. 'Dezzy boy, for a moment I thought I'd lost you! You gave me a right old shock!'

I felt down around his mouth but there was no toy. I was baffled and then I wondered, had I thrown it so hard that it'd sailed over the back of the fence?

Impossible, I thought shaking my head.

But Dez wasn't moving, so where was the toy? I dropped down onto my hands and knees and started to feel my way across the garden. The damp earth soaked up through the knees of my denim of my jeans but it didn't bother me. I was more worried about planting an open hand in some dog mess. Dez followed me, no doubt with a quizzical look on his face. I could just imagine him thinking, *what the hell is he doing now?*

If anyone was looking into my garden they would've thought I was a right nutter. I was on my hands and knees 'looking' for a squeaky toy with Dez trailing close behind wondering what on earth I was doing. It took a good fifteen minutes, but I found the toy and it was right in the middle of the garden exactly where I'd thrown it. Dez was just too bone idle to go and fetch it and now he was letting me know. He wasn't just a silly pooch I could keep entertained with a cheap squeaky toy, Dez was a highly-trained, intelligent animal and if I wanted the toy back, then I'd have to go and fetch it myself.

I realised then that Dez wasn't an ordinary dog, he was a character with a unique personality all of his own. Now he was letting me know that he wasn't going to waste his time doing silly things.

I sighed, dusted myself down and began to laugh. He'd obviously got bored after the first two throws. It tickled me because I'd spent my entire life asserting my authority yet here I was, both master and servant to this beautiful lad. It was bonkers!

The phone rang constantly, everyone wanted to meet the man himself and, even though they'd not actually seen him, Dez already had his own fan club of family and friends building up. I had to be firm but fair.

'I'm sorry but we're not accepting visitors this weekend,' I told them all. 'Dez needs to settle in.'

I'd turned into an over-protective dad but if truth be known, I knew what a softie Dez was and what a big heart he had. If he could fall in love with a schmuck like me then he'd fall for anyone! A selfish part of me didn't want him being smitten with anyone, not until we'd had time to develop our own special bond.

By the second evening Dez was exhausted and so was I. We'd even managed to establish some ground rules along the way too. Dez had not only become my companion but my shadow too and I learned to walk with my hands right out in front of me to check where he was so I didn't trip over him. We were learning together.

As teatime arrived I walked over to the spot in the kitchen where I kept 'the box'. Dez rushed off into the corner because he knew what was coming. He knew exactly what the sound of the cardboard food box scraping against the work surface meant. He remained there as still as a statue until the food was in his bowl. He stayed seated until I told him he could eat. It sounds regimented but that's how guide dogs are trained. It starts almost as soon as the pup is able to stand and the first lesson is to teach them not to eat until a whistle blows. It's just the beginning but it makes all the difference. Using the whistle helps train them to take commands. They need to do this when they start their guide dog training, which they start for real at around 12 months old. They have to learn how to obey commands because in the outside world a guide dog can't ever be distracted because it could mean the difference between life and death. Dogs like Dez don't even pass their full training until they're at least 18 months old. That's when they're matched up with a prospective owner. Emma explained that they do this by matching every-thing from walking speed to environment and personality. Poor old Dez must've drawn the short straw at doggy camp because he was matched with me! Joking aside, I knew that Emma had matched us well because she knew we were both so desperate to please one another.

'It's a good job you can't see his eyes,' Emma laughed after she'd dropped him off that first night.

I was puzzled and asked what she meant.

'Dez is like you John,' she laughed. 'He wears his heart on his sleeve and he has the most expressive face.'

I smiled at the thought.

I heard Dez scamper to his food bowl. However, I'd obviously kept him waiting a minute too long because I slipped on something: his drool all over the floor! Lesson one and two, don't walk around the flat in stocking feet and, whatever you do, don't keep Dez waiting for his food. He devoured the lot in seconds because he didn't believe in chewing up his food. After his dinner, Dez did his usual hoovering up against the floor searching for bonus crumbs.

'That's your lot mate,' I apologised.

I was almost grateful I couldn't see his big brown eyes because I know I'd have buckled and fed him more. My heart went out to him: I knew exactly how he felt because I'd battled my own weight issues when I'd ballooned to 16 stone. But now I'd got my act together, I was three stone lighter and I felt and guessed I looked a whole lot better. A new fitter and slimmer John had emerged and I didn't want Dez to go down the same slippery slope.

'It's a good job I can't see those big brown eyes,' I chuckled placing his box of food way out of reach.

He'd have gobbled down the lot if I'd let him. I felt his face push against my hand, pleading with me to change my mind.

'No Dez,' I said standing my ground. 'It's no good creeping

around me. What if Emma comes back on Monday and sees crumbs around your mouth? We'll both be for the high-jump!'

I grinned back at him but I'm sure Dez didn't appreciate the joke.

I won't tell if you won't I could almost hear him say.

Later, I was on the sofa when Dez jumped up for a cuddle. No dogs on the furniture, Emma had told me. Another rule broken, but I didn't care. I just pulled him in closer and hugged him for all I was worth.

'You've changed my life already Dez, do you know that?' I whispered in his ear.

Dez let out a sigh as if to say, *Whatever Dad, just don't forget to keep stroking the back of my ear and we'll be just fine.*

I almost wept with happiness. This dog had made me go completely soft in the head. Just as I started to wonder what I'd become, I felt something wet and warm slurp against my ear: a big Dezzy kiss. It seemed he felt exactly the same. Dez's weight shifted as he climbed off my lap and jumped down onto the floor. His paws padded against laminate and I heard a heavy sigh as he flopped down into his bed. I stood up and wandered over towards him. His fur felt soft and short behind the back of his ear and he leaned on me appreciatively as I stroked it. I cuddled him some more. He stretched out and I could feel his head as he rested it on top of his paws and sighed heavily through his nose. His body began to relax and I guessed he was falling asleep. Then he started to snore loudly, like a man who'd had too much to drink. Blimey, I wasn't expecting such a loud snorer! With Dez fast asleep, I wrapped a loving arm across his back and laid my head against the floor. Hours later, I woke as stiff as a board and cold. At first, I was disorientated but as I felt around me I realised what I'd done: I'd curled up and fallen asleep on the floor right next to Dez.

You soppy git, I smiled to myself. *What on earth had this dog done to me?*

The following morning was Sunday. As usual, Dez was sitting beside his food bowl as though he was awaiting his last ever meal but as I opened up the bin I realised it was full.

'I'm just nipping outside Dez,' I said telling him my movements as if he was my wife.

I couldn't let him out with me, not until Emma said it was okay to do so. I'd spent my life disobeying everyone but he was so precious I was certain I wasn't going to mess this up.

I grabbed the bin liner between my fingers and twisted it into a knot at the top. Holding it in my hand I headed for the door but felt something close beside me, it was Dez.

'No, mate, you can't. I'm really sorry,' I insisted.

His head tilted upwards against my hand and I knew he was looking up at me. I was just thankful that I couldn't see his heartbroken face.

'I'll be a minute I promise. I'm just taking this to the bin outside,' I explained.

Dez sat back down and sighed as if in a huff. I closed the door behind me and nipped out to the bin. I must've been gone for a total of ten seconds, but as soon as I walked back in through the door he bounced around like Tigger on Red Bull. There was no stopping him!

'Whoa!' I burst out laughing as he whizzed past me and back again. His tail whipped against my legs as he pushed past.

'Good grief Dez! Anyone would think I'd been gone six months, I've only been out to the bin!'

MY BOY

By the end of our long weekend, my best pal and I had spent 60 wonderful hours together. When Emma arrived on Monday morning she knew we had a bond that could never be broken. Wild horses wouldn't drag me away from Dez now. We were a team – a winning combination. We were Dez and John, and nothing or no one would ever tear us apart.

CHAPTER FIFTEEN

Madhouse

O N MONDAY MORNING the front door intercom buzzed.

'Hi John,' a chirpy voice piped up. 'It's Emma.'

I was so excited because I wanted her to see how well Dezzy Boy and I had bonded.

'Aww,' she sighed as soon as she stepped inside my flat. 'I can see you two have been getting on really well.'

It was bright and early, only 8.30am, but Dez and I were keen to start work. I'd been up since the crack of dawn anyway, Dez had seen to that, but it didn't matter because now, with this ball of energy bouncing beside me, I had a new lease of life and I was ready to take on the world. The first bit of training wasn't too taxing for old Dez, all he had to do was stand there looking pretty. This bit was down to me because, before we could even venture outside, I had to learn how to fasten his harness on. To be honest, putting the contraption

205

on would be hard enough for a fully-sighted person but as a blind man, just trying to get it the right way up was a challenge in itself because it all had to be fastened and secured into place with an underbelly strap using touch alone.

'Sorry Dez,' I apologised as I accidently knocked him against the side of his head. I could just imagine him tutting.

Come on, hurry up and get on with it Dad!

The more I fumbled and twisted the strap, the clumsier I became. Soon, I was all fingers and thumbs.

'Don't be too hard on yourself John,' Emma coaxed. 'It's tricky; it takes some getting used to.'

But I was impatient. I wanted to run before I could walk because I just couldn't wait to get out into the world and show off Dez.

'I think this is worse than taking my driving test,' I sighed as I struggled for the umpteenth time.

Suddenly, my fingers located the other end of the strap and hey presto, everything clicked into place.

'That's it, you've done it John. Well done!'

I did a quick check on Dez. I'd put it on properly and not managed to lock him in back to front or upside down! With a full heart I clipped on his lead triumphantly.

'Great! Now, let's do it again,' Emma said.

My heart sank. I had to know this off by heart but it was tedious and repetitive work. I could almost hear Dez huff. All he wanted to do was go outside and explore too.

But if I thought the harness was a challenge, then walking down the steps outside my flat was like picking my way through a war zone. Dez was eager and desperate to please, so together we were a bundle of nerves because we both wanted to get it right first time. Thankfully, Emma had a real skill;

she sensed our fear and soon put us at ease. If I thought it'd be like a driving test it was nothing in comparison to being led on a lead by Dez. He was an absolute star and obeyed all the rules but try as I might, it felt totally alien being 'dragged' along by a dog. I tried desperately, but my hand kept on shooting out in front of me more times than I care to admit.

'You need to relax,' Emma insisted.

I knew she was right and although I'd done a few practice walks with Dez, Volley and Morris, it's hard to put your trust in an animal when you can't see a thing in front of you. I trusted Dez with my life but there was still some fear kicking around the back of my subconscious. I tried my best to walk at a normal pace but I became disorientated and shuffled along; scared that I'd stumble or knock into something. On a few occasions I did actually trip up. I reckon Dez thought he'd landed himself with a right old beginner, someone who needed learner plates pinned to his back. I could hear him, huffing and complaining.

I've trained hard for months and come top of my class, for this old schmuck!

We only walked to the corner of the street but it may as well have been a ten-mile trek. I felt emotionally drained as it took all the concentration I had just to put one foot in front of the other. At one point we stopped for a breather when Emma began to laugh.

'What?' I asked turning towards her.

'Oh John,' she said. 'It's Dez. I can almost tell what he's thinking because he keeps raising his eyebrows up and down.'

I laughed because she didn't have to tell me. Dez was a real character, not a robot. I could just imagine him moaning about me, rolling his eyes.

Blimey, they've matched me with a right one here.

I was still smiling as I dipped down gave him a loving pat on his head. He soon forgot his huff and nuzzled in gratefully.

'It's okay Dez,' I chuckled. 'I know I've got a long way to go but with you leading me there I know we're gonna make it.'

His wet tongue licked the back of my hand affectionately. The feeling was mutual and in that moment I knew we were going to be okay. Emma had chosen well. Dez was a character but then, so was I. We were a match made in heaven.

After four or five hours, we said goodbye to Emma as she packed up the harness and took it away with her. It is part of the guide dog training that all mobility instructors take away the harness at the end of the day in case you feel tempted to go out on your own, which would put both yourself and your dog at risk. It's only handed over when you've completed your training. Despite my dodgy past, I was never once tempted to break the rules. Dez meant the world to me and I would never put him in danger.

Although we'd had our walk through my little village of Almondsbury, I wasn't done yet.

'Come on Dez, we need to go over a few commands.' I said sounding like a teacher, getting back up to my feet.

Dez was tired but I felt him zip up to standing position because he was thinking one thing and one thing only.

Great! Are there any biscuits in it for me?

There were, but only a few.

I stood up in the lounge and patted him on the head.

'Stay Dez,' I ordered as I began to walk over to the other side of the room. Dez did exactly as he was told and stood as still as a statue. I called his name and a split second later he came bounding over towards me.

'Good boy,' I said patting him on the head. 'Well done!'

Biscuit? Dez insisted nudging his nose against my hand. How could I refuse?

'Go on, just one then, but don't tell Emma!' I whispered in his ear.

This time I was prepared for his drool and kept my shoes on. I'd learned my lesson, no more slippy shocks in stocking feet. After a half an hour of practising commands I felt completely knackered and flopped back down onto the sofa. Dez jumped up with me and I ignored the rules. Dez wasn't a dog, he was my boy. I wrapped an arm around his neck and pulled him closer for a cuddle.

'I'll be better at walking tomorrow, I promise.'

My hand slid down along his back but it was too late, he wasn't listening anymore. He'd gone, off to the world of slumber. His snores gave him away. I rested my head against a pillow and drifted off into a blissful sleep. I felt content with Dez beside me – my dark and shallow existence was a thing of the past. Dez had brought fun and sunshine into my life and I radiated and basked in its warmth.

The following day, Emma returned and this time we ventured a little further into the village. We practised each of my regular routes again and again until it started to feel familiar. The local shop was on my main route. I tentatively stepped outside and with Emma by my side and the harness in my hand we set off. Dez walked in front of us but on my left hand side. He expertly guided me along the narrow country pavements towards the corner store. Unlike other shops, our village store is run by local residents and it's quite a success. It was a cold October day when we walked in through the door. I was looking forward to speaking to my friends at the shop but, as soon as we entered we were greeted by a film crew. They were from the local TV station and there was a reporter doing a piece to camera.

'Sorry,' I muttered as I stumbled in through the door with a clatter.

It was obvious from the conversation she was busy doing an interview. But the reporter was lovely and didn't mind my interruption, in fact she even asked if I was a regular user of the store.

'I am,' I told her proudly. 'It's been a lifesaver for me because as you can see I'm blind, but I shop here all the time because it's right on my doorstep.'

Suddenly, Dez nudged in between us. He'd seen me talking to a young lady and wasn't going to let me get all the attention.

'And who's this?' she said kneeling down to give Dez a stroke. He lapped it up gratefully.

'This is Dez, my guide dog. We're on one of our first practice walks together.' I told her although I guessed it must've been obvious to anyone who'd seen me shuffling up the path.

'Would you mind if I interview you for a piece?'

'Me?' I asked a little taken aback.

Dez nudged against my leg as if urging me to do it.

'Of course,' I replied. 'No problem.'

Five minutes later, a camera panned in on me as the reporter asked for my thoughts on the community-run shop. The shop is the hub of our village and something that, along with Dez, had helped give me my life back. There had been many days when I'd just popped into say hello to the ladies behind the counter. There was even a coffee shop at the back where I'd often sit down for a drink. It had not only helped introduce me to my neighbours, it had also helped build my confidence, so much so that I was out socialising every day.

I felt a tug on the lead as Dez rose to his feet and started sniffing out possible food opportunities closer to him on the floor.

'So John,' the reporter began. 'Tell me what this community store means to you.'

'Well, it feels like a social occasion when I come in. I often stop and have a coffee and I've got to know members of staff – I'm on first name terms with them. It's lovely here because it's so personal,' I explained, trying my best to concentrate and look forward.

If I thought the camera was on me then I was sorely mistaken because as soon as we'd finished I heard stifled giggles from behind the counter. Dez was at it again. The cameraman had caught him breaking into the back of the shot snuffling around jars of sweets desperate to try a few. His Labrador nose had sniffed them out; jellybeans and yoghurt-covered raisins, if only he could get the lids off with his paws! My new pal had just become a TV star and I'd known him less than a week!

'I think he's hungry,' someone chuckled.

'Dez?' I grinned. 'He's always hungry, he's a Labrador – it's an occupational hazard!'

My Dez the TV star. It was a premonition of what was yet to come.

CHAPTER SIXTEEN

Never Look Back

TV STARDOM HAD GONE to Dez's head but if he had any ideas of grandeur then there was someone much more majestic waiting in the wings to knock him off his showbiz perch.

Emma, our mobility instructor, was busy training another dog alongside Dez – a small German Shepherd bitch called Gwyn. From day one, Gwyn made it clear that she considered Dez to be somewhat beneath her. Emma laughed whenever the two of them were together in the back of the car.

'She's doing it again,' she chuckled. 'Dez is all over Gwyn like a rash but she simply doesn't want to know. She's pretending he's not there, sticking her nose up in the air.'

I laughed as I imagined grand Lady Gwyn dressed in her white gloves and sparkly tiara mixing with the working-class Lab in the back. Gwyn was gorgeous but quite the little princess.

'What's she doing now?' I asked as the dogs jumped out onto the pavement.

'She's turned her back on him, but Dez is trying his best to impress her.'

We both started to laugh. It was comical as Emma started to give me a running commentary of the body language between the lady and my very own tramp. No matter how hard Dez tried, little Gwyn would always burst his bubble with one of her withering looks. She was a beautiful and talented guide dog but she really thought she was it compared to my boy.

Some people naturally assume that guide dogs are just robots. I did and so did my family and friends – but that was before I got Dez. All dogs have their own individual personalities and just because they're highly intelligent animals who are trained to precision, it doesn't mean they don't retain their own character traits. But if Gwyn was a lady then Dez was almost certainly a lad about town. He's got such a big personality that I could just imagine him hanging around with his mates, chatting up the ladies. If Gwyn was a princess living in a castle, then Dez was almost certainly the local oik from the council estate, much like his owner.

'Is she looking down her nose at him again?' I asked Emma a little later even though it was obvious.

Emma laughed and confirmed that Gwyn was.

'Hey, I'll have you know lady, that my Dez is a TV star,' I told Gwyn as she trotted with her nose in the air alongside us.

I felt Dez's head look up at me.

That's right Dad, you tell her. At least I'm famous!

I gave him a pat, knelt down and undid his harness and

then he was off with Lady Gwyn, running free on open land. Once the leads were off so were Dez and Gwyn with all the class boundaries forgotten. Now they were just two pups running off into the distance. Gwyn had taken off her white gloves and her tiara was back in its box. They were just regular dogs running free against the wind.

'They love each other really,' Emma commented as she watched them run.

'I reckon our Gwyn has got a secret soft spot for old Dez.' I said leaning in, nudging her against the arm.

Emma and I stood there for ages. I couldn't see but I could picture them jumping around and playing as happy and free as children.

'He's changed my life, you know.' I whispered confidentially to Emma.

A bout of emotion choked up and stuck at the back of my throat. In that moment I felt overwhelmed with love for Dez.

'I know,' Emma whispered back. 'I know he has John.'

Before long, Dez and I were getting better with each passing day. Instead of stumbling or tripping I was able to hold my head high and walk along with confidence. I'm sure many of the good residents of Almondsbury saw us on our travels but no one ever stopped or interrupted our training because they knew just how important it was to me.

As my confidence grew, Emma took us further afield to other villages including Thornbury, and my old stomping ground of Frampton Cotterell. Each time, I could almost hear the cogs in Dez's brain ticking away as he made mental notes on the best and safest routes. With Emma there to guide us, we learnt as a team how to get on and off a bus to travel to our destinations. Before long, Dez had mastered it so well that he was getting up one stop before on the bus just to warn me that the next one was ours.

'How does he know how to do that?' I asked Emma in astonishment.

'He's watching and waiting all the time,' she explained. 'He's taking everything in: sounds, smells, and the routine.'

I shook my head in amazement. Dez wasn't just a dog, he was a genius! But he wasn't alone; there are thousands of other guide dogs doing this day in, day out.

Soon, everything started to slot into place. When his harness was on, Dez was the ultimate professional, always watching and waiting. He wasn't reckless or impatient; instead he'd err on the side of caution, anything to keep me safe. However, as soon as the brace was removed he was off duty and back to being a regular dog and a bouncing ball of fun and energy.

After four weeks, we'd reached the end of the road. We were almost fully trained. Emma had done a fantastic job, especially with me. Dez already knew his stuff but he'd adapted everything he'd learned to fit around me. From now on this wonderful creature would be my eyes on the world and all it had to offer.

Finally, the day arrived when it was make or break – our qualifying walk – akin to taking a driving test at the end of training. Only today, there wouldn't be just one pair of eyes watching us but two. Emma had been joined by her boss Alun, and now it was up to us to convince him that we were ready and able. Butterflies rose and fluttered inside the pit of my stomach as we set off alone and without guidance. I knew we were being monitored and closely scrutinised in case Dez put a paw wrong or made a fatal error but I knew he wouldn't, he was my Dez, I knew he'd do me proud.

It was a familiar route and one we'd walked many times before; the journey to Bob and Kath's house. They were my friends and one of the couples who had pulled me out of my pit of despair in the early days. In my mind's eye I knew this journey like the back of my hand and so did Dez but unbeknown to me, roadwork barriers were blocking our path. They'd been in the middle of the road but someone or something had knocked them over and now they were scattered everywhere making it impossible for us to pass. Unable to see, I didn't know the danger was coming but Dez did. With Emma and Alun watching it was imperative that he made the right decision for both of us. In my mind I'd prepared for the usual – the off-kerb obstacle – because I knew it was coming. The barriers were in the road, I told myself, and Dez knew to swerve to the side of them. I was walking but also waiting and counting down the moment until we needed to veer to the left. When we didn't, I was worried that Dez had missed it or done something wrong. But then I remembered Emma's mantra and now it was ringing in my ears.

Go with your dog. Trust Dez.

So I did. Dez came to a halt just short of the obstacle and waited by the kerb. I could sense his head looking up watching out for traffic. We paused for a moment as I waited to see what he would do next.

'Find your way Dez,' I encouraged.

I knew Dez, and if he was going a different route then there was a good reason for it. My shoes tapped against the tarmac of the road as Dez expertly picked his way around the littered pathway and into the edge of the road. I listened out for cars but I knew I was in safe paws.

A few moments later, we were back up on the path as step by step, he led me right up to my friend's front door. Emma was choked with emotion when Alun told us we'd passed. I was elated and punched the air with delight. We'd done it! When she told me how Dez had cleverly picked his way through the debris, never once putting me in danger, I hugged him for all I was worth.

'It was a gold badge moment – Dez was magnificent – you both were,' she said proudly.

'A genius as well as a TV star!' I laughed, snuggling into the side of Dez's face. But he took it all in his stride: all in a day's work for my clever boy.

Afterwards, back at my flat Emma handed me something. The metal felt cold against my fingers as she placed the harness in the palm of my hand.

'That's it John, congratulations!' she said patting me on the side of my arm.

I felt proud of myself but most of all, I felt proud of Dez. It was a truly wonderful moment. Before, I'd followed a bad path in life but now, thanks to Dez, I was not only on the right one but on my way up too.

'The hard work starts now!' Emma said, breaking my thoughts.

I nodded gratefully. It was down to this woman and her wonderful organisation that I could live once more. Before I'd lost my sight, I'd taken my life for granted but not anymore. Thanks to Emma, all her hard work, patience and belief in me, I'd come through the other side. She was and still is one-in-a-million – a truly unique and amazing person who has tirelessly worked to improve the quality of many people's lives.

'I don't know how to thank you,' I said humbly as we headed over to the door.

'You don't have to thank me, John,' she said. 'I'll be coming back to see you and Dez but if you need anything, just call.'

After she'd left it was just Dez and me. In many ways it felt like an anti-climax after being on such a high.

'Well, mate. We did it.' I said giving him a cuddle. Dez nestled in against me but I knew what he was thinking.

Well, what are we waiting for?

With nothing to hold us back I put on the harness and off we went, back to the community shop to share the good news. The ladies were all over Dez like a rash but I didn't mind, he'd earned it! Anyway, by now he was used to the attention. He'd become an overnight sensation in our little village and everyone who knew him, loved him. Of course, he lapped it up. Dez is a real character but he's also a complete softie and, just like me, crumbles when it comes to the opposite sex. My Dez, the Barry White of the dog world! Mean, dark, moody and terribly romantic. On the rare occasion he did bark, and it was rare, he would make a deep throaty sound just like the singer himself.

Of course, it wasn't long before my lovely pal caught the eye of the neighbourhood female pooches and by the time his birthday arrived, he received three times as many cards as I did. In the end, mine seemed so sparse that I put them alongside Dez's cards on the mantelpiece to pad them out a bit. Typical, my dog was more popular than me!

The same thing happened when it came to Valentine's

Day. When three cards popped through the letterbox and landed on my doormat I thought my luck was in. I sat there preening myself as a friend opened them up one by one and read them aloud. For a split second I wondered who my army of female admirers were but my ego was soon popped when I heard that all three were for the man himself, Mr Dez. I felt him grinning as he sat and listened.

See, Dad. Told you I'm better looking than you!

Dez had become so popular that a simple walk now took a few hours. The more we walked the more friends we made on our way as Dez and his killer brown eyes drew them in, one by one.

One afternoon before I'd got Dez, I was walking through the village using my long cane when a lady spotted me. Her name was Fiona; she was a doctor and popular member of the village who is married to an equally marvellous man called Ian. Fiona watched from afar as I negotiated my way along the narrow pavement tapping my cane as I went. She could tell I found it awkward. She watched but didn't like to approach because she could see I was deep in concentration and didn't want to put me off my stride. A few weeks later, she saw me again, only this time I had Dez. Not long afterwards, Fiona organised a charity string quartet concert in the village church. It had been a long time since I'd been inside a church but I went along to support the event. Dez sat patiently at my side as Fiona came over. She was a warm and friendly woman and we soon got chatting.

'I've seen you with Dez,' she explained. 'I wondered if you'd both like to come out with me and my dog Isla?'

A warm rush of gratitude washed over me because I knew it'd be good for Dez and for me.

'Yes, we'd love that,' I said gratefully.

The following day we tagged along with Fiona and Isla. We got on famously but not as much as Dez and Isla – he was smitten! After that, we became good mates and would regularly take the lovebirds out together. I thought how much my life had turned around in such a short space of time. Before now, I'd hung around with thugs and petty thieves but now here I was in the company of doctors, surgeons and decent folk. Dez had saved me in many more ways than one. To lead a strong character you need to have a strong character and lots of personality and it was clear my Dez had that in bucket loads.

During our training, we learned lots of familiar routes, one of them being a path through the local shopping centre. One afternoon, we were walking through the centre when I heard a toddler's voice cry out in surprise. I waited but Dez didn't even break his step so I knew there was nothing to worry about. Moments later, I felt a gentle tap on my shoulder. I turned to the voice of a woman, a young mother who had chased after us to catch us up.

'Excuse me,' she said, a little breathless.

'Yes,' I replied turning to face her.

'I'm sorry to bother you but your dog has got, er, well, he's got a lollipop sticking out of his mouth!'

My feet froze to the floor. Was this a wind up?

'What?' I gasped.

'Your dog,' she repeated. She was trying her best but by now she couldn't contain her laughter.

'It's your dog he's... he's got a lollipop in his mouth. Oh, he does look funny!' she sniggered and with that she dissolved into fits of laughter. By now I sensed others had stopped to watch. I heard laughter all around me as I dipped down towards Dez's mouth. I ran my fingers along the velvety fur of his mouth until...sure enough, there it was: a lollipop stick sticking straight out of the front of his mouth. Now that I was closer I could smell it too, it was strawberry flavoured! I gave the stick a tug but Dez wasn't letting go. It was his lollipop and if he wanted to suck it, he would. I heard his tongue moving around as he slurped on it. The laughter became louder as more people stopped to watch the dog with the lolly.

'What the? Dez!' I scolded.

I wrapped my fingers around the end of the stick and I gave it a good yank. There was some resistance on the other end but I finally managed to extract the lolly from his mouth.

'Dez!' I huffed. His head bowed in shame.

He knew he couldn't eat when he was on duty... but sweets! Suddenly, a thought occurred to me.

'Where on earth did he get it from?' I asked the woman. The lolly was sticky with Dez's dribble and now it was all over my fingertips, it felt disgusting.

'My daughter,' the woman chuckled. 'That's what I was trying to tell you. She was in her pushchair waving her lolly about but he must have thought it was a present for him.'

I covered my mouth with horror. It was worse than I thought, Dez had stolen it! He was a guide dog and a thief!

'Your little girl, is she alright?'

'Oh yeah,' the woman replied, her giggles subsiding. 'She's fine. I'm always telling her not to wave sweets about but you know what kids are like, they never listen!'

I knew exactly what she meant. I was standing with a big kid on a lead right now.

'But you,' she said patting Dez on the back, 'you are gorgeous!'

It was clear the young mum didn't care. Dez must've flashed his big brown eyes at her but I was mortified, Dez the lollipop thief!

'Listen, I'm so sorry. I don't know what got into him... I mean, he's normally so good.' I said, trying to apologise.

'Here,' I said thrusting a hand deep into the front pocket of my jeans. 'Take this, so that you can buy her another one.'

I held out a note in my hand and tried to push it into the woman's hand but she refused.

'Ten pounds? No way! I could buy a thousand lollies with that! No,' she insisted. 'I'm not cross, it was really funny. You should've seen the look on my little girl's face. He's quite a character your dog.'

'He is that,' I said as I flushed pink with embarrassment. 'Well, if you won't accept £10, let me give you this.'

The pound coin felt heavy and chunky between my fingers but the woman refused that too.

'No, it's fine.'

'Please,' I begged. I was mortified Dez had disgraced himself publicly and I told him so. But he wasn't bothered; he just wanted his lolly back.

'Take it,' I said pressing the coin into the young mum's hand.

'Okay,' she sighed, 'but only if it makes you feel better.'

My face was scarlet with embarrassment and I couldn't get out of the shopping centre fast enough. The cold air outside cooled my face but I still couldn't get over it. I turned to Dez who I hoped was hanging his head in shame.

'Who do you think you are?' I asked. 'Bloody Kojak?'

'Forward,' I said as he got up to his feet and we headed back home.

The following day I invited a friend over. I was so horrified by the lollipop incident that I asked her to bring her toddler and pushchair along so I could teach Dez right from wrong. We moved the coffee table to one side and practised walking past her little girl, who was holding a delicious lolly in her hand.

'No Dez,' I scolded him the first time as we walked past because I felt his head lift up so that his nose could sniff the air.

We spent the afternoon practising until I was certain I'd cured his light-fingered ways.

'I think I've cured him of his addiction,' I told my friend who thought it was all very amusing. But deep down, I knew Dez would always have a sweet tooth.

Before long I saw the funny side. It was ironic that of all the guide dogs in the country, I'd been matched with a light-fingered pooch, one almost as light-fingered as me in my youth. But I'd seen the error of my ways and now, if I was going to keep my Dez on the straight and narrow, I'd have to lead by example.

To be fair it was Dez's only misdemeanour and, sweets aside, his character and behaviour had been impeccable. When we were on a walk, Dez was the Green Cross Code man, or dog. If anything, he was such a worrier that he'd have me waiting half an hour longer than everyone else just to double then triple check that the coast was clear.

One day, we were walking along when the kerb dipped down and trailed off without warning. It was a narrow country path so I hadn't realised and inadvertently stepped out into the road. As quick as a flash I felt a body in front of me. It was as solid as a rock and stopped me dead in my tracks blocking my way. It was Dez. He'd seen the danger and reacted quickly. Thankfully, there was nothing coming but I knew this was a big deal for Dez. The Green Cross Code dog had just broken his golden rule and stepped into the road just to stop me from falling into the path of a car. He'd put himself in danger to protect me. I realised what a star he truly was not just on TV, but in day to day life. My heart was pounding ten to the dozen with fear but I was so proud of him.

'Good boy,' I rewarded him but the incident made me worry.

The thought of anything happening to my precious Dez sickened me. I wanted to look after him and I felt frustrated that he had to do the lion's share of the work. Our bond had deepened with every day. I knew this wonderful four-legged creature had been sent down from heaven to look after me. Dez was my right arm and the apple of my eye, but as it turned out, I wasn't alone.

With the Queen's Diamond Jubilee celebrations upon us, the village held a fete. As a special one-off, the organisers staged a beauty pageant not for girls, but for dogs. There was some stiff competition yet despite them all, Dez only had eyes for one lady, his doggy sweetheart Isla. She was a black flat-coated retriever who overnight had become his walking pal, long-term girlfriend and general love of his life – the feeling was mutual. Over the months, Dez had built up a small army of admirers but his heart belonged to Isla. She was a hot favourite in the competition so, when she won, Dez and I cheered and jigged around like lunatics. She coolly strutted over afterwards to say 'hello' and Dez was beside himself. As the lovebirds mingled against the crowds suddenly a thought occurred to me. I turned to Fiona and Ian.

'Hey, does that mean I can tell everyone that my Dez is going out with a beauty queen?'

We all burst out laughing. All except Dez, who was far too busy romancing his special lady.

However, there was another woman in the wings waiting to get her claws into Dez and her name was Jangle. She belonged to Monica, from Guide Dogs, and she was another black flat-coated retriever. Dez clearly had a 'type'. Sure enough, on Valentine's Day a card from Jangle arrived along with the others through my letterbox. One was from my nieces, whilst another was posted by an anonymous admirer. Dez had become the heartthrob of Almondsbury, and I was thrilled, if not a little peeved.

'Hey, mate. You need to start sharing these women out,' I laughed. 'You can't keep them all to yourself you know.'

Sure enough, Dez soon repaid the favour as mystery women soon started to approach me too. But they weren't really interested in me, only Dez.

'Isn't he gorgeous?' a lady swooned as she passed by us in a coffee shop one day.

'Oh, I love Labradors and your dog is so cute. What's his name?' another asked.

I grinned as more and more women popped over to make friends with Dez. He was quite a babe magnet when he put his mind to it. After a while he became oblivious to his women-pulling qualities but I loved it!

'Yes, he's great isn't he?' I'd say striking up conversation. 'Pleased to meet you, I'm John by the way.'

Being blind has many drawbacks, and one is not being able

to tell if a woman is single or not. Without being able to slyly look, I'd hold my right hand out to shake and feel their left hand for a wedding ring instead. Sneaky, I know, but a man's got to work with what he's got! Dez soon became my wingdog, ice-breaker and chat-up line all rolled in one but no one loved him loved him more than I did. One slight raise of his Roger Moore style 007 eyebrows and ladies would melt all around us. Mind you, if any blokes came near I'd soon brush them off. Instead of a chat I'd reply with monosyllabic answers, I couldn't have them cramping mine and Dez's style.

As nice as it was, the attention wasn't always welcome. One afternoon Dez and I were on a long and rather tedious train journey when a young lady sat down in the seat next to me and started to chat. She began with my favourite subject, Dez.

'I love your dog, what's he called?' she said.

I sat up and started telling her all about my wonder dog. She was a friendly soul but after ten minutes of her recounting her entire life-story, I started to think that maybe things weren't quite what they seemed.

As it happened, I was bursting for the loo so I asked the young lady if she'd find the train guard for me.

'Why?' she replied.

'Because I need to go to the loo, so I need him to show me where it is.'

'No problem,' she said jumping straight to her feet. 'Link my arm, I'll take you.'

I was so desperate that I accepted her offer and followed her along the crowded train. After a few more moments of light chitchat we arrived at the cubicle. It was a space-pod type of affair, one where the door whooshes open at the press of a button. I was just about to step inside with Dez when I felt someone close behind us.

'Want some help in here?' a voice whispered in my ear.

I was mortified.

'Er, no, thanks. I think I'll manage.' I mumbled, flushing bright red with horror.

I waited longer than normal to make sure the coast was clear but as soon as I pressed the door open, there she was again.

'I wondered where you'd got to.' She giggled grabbing my arm.

To say I felt intimidated was an understatement and, I'm sure she meant well even if she was a little overenthusiastic. Once back in my seat she chatted some more until the guard announced the next station.

'This is me,' she said sadly.

Inwardly, I sighed with relief. I'd never been much good with women because underneath it all I'm still a little old-fashioned and a forceful woman like her scared the hell out of me. Not that Dez cared. He was glad of the extra fuss and attention. I was only grateful he couldn't talk for real, otherwise I reckon he'd have offered her our full address and phone number.

'Here,' she said getting to her feet. I heard the tell-tale crumple of a piece of paper as she pushed it deep into the top pocket of my jacket.

'There,' she said patting my chest.

Her voice dipped as she whispered into my ear.

'It's got my telephone number on it. Call me.'

I was so stunned, I didn't know what to say but within seconds she'd gone. I sighed with relief and, when I was quite sure the train had pulled away from the station, I took out the piece of paper and slipped it surreptitiously down the side of my seat. As I did so, a peal of laughter rang out from the seat opposite.

'You should have seen your face,' a fellow traveller chuckled. 'It was a picture, especially when she put her number in your top pocket.'

I grinned and started to laugh.

'That's nothing,' I told him cupping my hand up against the side of my mouth to stop others from listening. 'She wanted to follow me into the toilet!'

The man roared with laughter.

'It must be the dog, he draws them in.'

'Too right!' I nodded. 'Normally, he doesn't share them out but there's a few I wish he'd keep to himself.'

It was a surreal moment. Only a year before, I'd fretted that women would never look at me again, after all, what did I have to offer? But I'd been proved wrong yet again. Adam was right. He'd told me during those counselling sessions that women couldn't resist a blind fella. I hadn't believed him but now I did. I didn't even have to do anything. With Dez the babe magnet I had women quite literally throwing themselves right at me. I was a very lucky man indeed.

When I later recounted the story to my ex-wife Tracey she couldn't stop laughing.

Dez had a unique ability to woo the fairer sex on my behalf. Gone were those long awkward moments in pubs and clubs when I wondered what to do or say. I had Dez and now there was no looking back.

CHAPTER SEVENTEEN

Keep on Moving

NOW THAT I had Dez I felt on top of the world and together and nothing or no one could stop us.

A month or so after I qualified, I went along to a regional meeting of Guide Dogs. Like most people, I assumed the organisation received funding from the Government but it didn't. It's purely a charitable organisation staffed mainly by volunteers and run on the generosity and goodwill of the public. I was astonished at the costs: training and keeping a dog like Dez throughout his lifetime costs around £50,000.

The great thing about the Guide Dogs charity is not only does it give people their lives and freedom back, it also meets all the running costs too. Even though Dez was mine to keep, this amazing organisation provided his specialist food and paid for all his vet's bills too. The cost of training a dog like Dez is huge, approximately £400 per dog, per week at the training centre. I was gutted that I couldn't say thank you by donating a large wad of cash so I did the next best thing; I volunteered to become a fundraiser.

I'd already met Monica and Diana, the two main fund-raisers in my area at a meeting a month after I'd finished my training with Dez. I understood first-hand how much this little fella had turned my life around so when the call went out, Dez and I stepped forward.

'I want to get involved,' I insisted. 'I wouldn't even be here if it wasn't for Dez. I'll do anything I can to help.'

From that moment on my support for Guide Dogs was unwavering so, when they asked for volunteers outside the local store in Thornbury, I was the first to put up my hand. It was a cold day but standing in the foyer of the supermarket I knew we were making a difference, albeit in a very small way.

'Please give to Guide Dogs,' I said holding out the collection box in my hands.

Within minutes a woman wandered over towards me.

'Hello,' she said.

'Hello,' I replied before realising she wasn't actually talking to me but Dez.

'What a beautiful dog. What's his name?' she asked, turning her attentions back to me. But it wasn't long before she was all over the main man again.

'He's called Dez and he's my lifesaver.' I told her proudly.

Then something remarkable happened and, before I knew it, I'd started to tell this complete stranger what a difference Dez and Guide Dogs had made to my life.

'So, you only lost your sight recently?' She seemed a little shocked.

I nodded my head and swallowed hard. Emotion had risen up and lodged at the back of my throat. It had been one of the first times I'd spoken to anyone openly outside of my counselling sessions with Adam. Now that I had, I was shocked just how much it had affected me.

'What an incredible story and what an incredible dog,' the woman said, patting me warmly on the arm. 'You must be incredibly proud of him.'

'I am,' I said, blinking back the tears. I was grateful for my black glasses so that she couldn't see my watery eyes.

'Here,' she said putting something inside my collection box. I heard a series of chinks as one coin after another dropped.

'Thanks. I just want to help them because they've given me my life back and so has Dez. I'd be lost without him.'

I gave my pal a loving stroke across his back. His warm body turned in towards me so I kissed him on his big square head.

The woman said goodbye whilst I tried to pull myself back together.

You soppy sod, I could just imagine Dez thinking, rolling his eyes.

I laughed too: if only my tough old pals could see me now!

It wasn't long before another person approached and dropped more coins into the collection tin, and then another.

'I just had to come over,' a young mother insisted. 'It's your dog; as soon as I walked in he looked straight at me. I couldn't walk past without coming over to say hello. Is it okay if my son strokes him?'

'Yes, course it is,' I replied with a warm smile. 'Hey, Dez. Come and say hello to this little boy.'

Minutes later I was surrounded again.

'Your dog has the most expressive face I've ever seen. I just had to come over to say hello. Here, let me give you something.'

And so the pattern followed. It was only the local supermarket but Dez had caused quite a stir. Some of the other guide dogs became tired but not my Dez, he lapped it up, basking in the constant attention. He was quite the salesman too, making direct eye contact with every shopper who came through the door so that they felt obliged to put something in our tin. Although we stood there for hours, Dez never once got bored, instead he played to his audience. One look at those big brown eyes and the ladies soon came running. By the end of the afternoon our collection box was bursting: it had been an exceptional day.

So, when Diana asked us to attend another supermarket I readily agreed. Sure enough, Dez was at it again.

'Isn't he adorable?' one lady said.

'Isn't it clever how they train them? Amazing, I just don't know how they do it.' This sounded like an elderly man.

With all the wonderful feedback and comments I started to relax in my role as an official fundraiser. At last, I had a new purpose in life and it was to be here, making a difference with Dez. Hours later I felt a tap on my arm and instinctively turned around.

'Yes,' I replied into the darkness.

'Excuse me, would it be okay if I gave your dog a treat?' an old lady asked. I could tell she was a pensioner by the sound of her voice. By now, I was getting good at guessing people's ages from the words they used or how they spoke.

'Treats' was a bit of a dirty word in our house. I loved giving Dez treats as reward for good behaviour but the problem was he loved his treats a little too much and, after the lollipop incident, I was trying to keep him in check.

'Yes,' I told her, 'that's fine but please could you give it to me first and then I can give it to him in small amounts.'

The woman fell silent and, for a moment, I was worried I'd offended her but then I realised she was busy stroking Dezzy boy. He was up on all fours nuzzling against her, enjoying a good ear rub.

'Yes, yes, I will,' she said. 'I'll just pop inside now and see what I can find. You're a good boy, aren't you?'

I grinned thinking it was an odd thing to say but then I realised she was still talking to Dez. As soon as she left I felt him tug at the harness. It was too late; he'd already heard the word 'treat' and as usual, his eyes were bigger than his belly.

'No Dez,' I told him. 'Not yet.'

'Thank you,' I called after her but she'd already gone.

So many more people came over to meet Dez that afternoon that I'd almost forgotten about the old lady. However, I'm certain Dez was still keeping an eye out because as soon as he spotted her walking back over he jumped up and started wagging his tail.

'Look what I've got for you!' she said rattling a packet in her hand. Dez's body swayed from side to side as he furiously wagged his tail in anticipation.

'Here,' she said placing an oblong packet in the palm of my hand. The metallic wrapper felt a little different to normal so I was intrigued as to what it was she had bought him.

'Thank you, that's very kind,' I smiled wrapping my fingers around the packet.

'You're very welcome, and so are you,' she said ruffling the fur on top of Dez's head before turning to walk away. But then it struck me, I needed to know what it was she'd bought before she disappeared, so I called after her and asked.

'Oh, it's a Twix,' she replied.

I waited until the sound of her footsteps disappeared off into the distance. Once the coast was clear, I took the chocolate bar and pushed it deep down into my top jacket pocket where he couldn't reach it.

'No chance,' I told him. I could feel his big brown eyes looking up, burning into me and pleading with me to change my mind.

'No, you can't have it mate. It's chocolate: it could kill you.'

Dez huffed and slumped back down onto the floor in disgust but I could still sense him staring straight at me.

'Look mate, I can't have it either because I'm diabetic, so we're both stuffed!'

I knew he wasn't listening but thinking.

I love sweets, but you won't even share…

The woman was only trying to be kind but after that day I made it a rule to never to allow Dez to accept anything from a stranger without checking it first. Dez wasn't happy but I had to look out for him.

We did more and more supermarkets and got the same response from everyone we met.

'You're so brave. I don't know how I'd have coped.' People often said after hearing my story but I always brought the conversation back to Dez, because I wanted the attention to be on him and Guide Dogs – they were the real heroes.

Then Monica had another suggestion.

'We often go into schools, colleges and workplaces to spread the word, to tell people all about Guide Dogs. I just wondered if you'd like to get involved?'

'Like? I'd love to,' I told her.

A week or so later our first 'talk' had been arranged. I felt nervous but Monica and Diana reassured me saying I'd be fine.

'I'll get up and give a talk and then people will come over to you and Dez so they can meet a real-life guide dog. They may have questions but then again, they may not. Just tell them honestly what Dez has done for you,' Monica said talking me through.

She knew just how much I loved Dez, and how much I enjoyed talking about him. He was my favourite subject so this was right up my street.

'Where is it we're going?' I asked as we travelled with Diana in the car. We were on our way to one of the nominated workplaces.

'It's a distribution centre,' Monica explained. She said a name but it didn't mean anything to me.

'They're thinking of making Guide Dogs the company's charity of the year.'

'Great!' I replied. 'Good for them. If Dez can't convince them then I don't know who can.'

Dez must've pulled one of his faces because they both started to laugh and I joined in. For the first time in ages, I felt blissfully happy. I stretched out a hand for my pal and as I did I felt a wet nose sniff against it appreciatively.

'Your first real job, Dezzy boy,' I said ruffling his hair. 'Do it well and we could raise a fortune to pay for lots more dogs like you!'

The car pulled up and we all got out and headed over to the reception. We were directed to the staff canteen but as soon as we walked in the smell of cooked food caught Dez's attention. I heard him sniff as he lifted up his nose, savoured the air, and began to drool.

'It's not dinner time yet mate; we've got work to do.'

I turned to Monica and Diana. 'I'm really looking forward to this.' It was true, I was. I couldn't wait to get started.

A few minutes later we were sat talking when someone tapped me lightly on the shoulder. My dodgy past automatically made me flinch.

'Hello John,' a voice said. 'How you doing?'

'Hello,' I replied, wondering who on earth it was.

Suddenly, someone else spoke.

'Hello John, he said it was you. I can't believe it, how are you?'

I scratched my head.

Where the hell was I, and who were these people?

'You don't know who this is, do you John?' the first voice guessed correctly.

I shook my head. I didn't.

'Well,' he said turning to Monica and Diana. 'The last time I saw this man he was kicking seven shades of crap out of a fella here. Well done John!'

I gasped as his words hung in mid-air, wrapped in an awkward silence. But the man laughed heartily and patted his hand against my back. I felt the blood drain from my face but he was still laughing.

'Yeah, John only did what we all wanted to do. Don't worry mate, he left here a long time ago.'

I was mortified. My past had caught up with me and on my first proper job – I'd been bang to rights.

The second man said a name and that's when it all fell into place. I was at my old workplace; the one where I'd hammered the man in the toilet after he'd come at me in a forklift truck. I budged up in my seat as the pair sat down beside me and explained how the old company had been bought out by a bigger firm, hence the name change. That's why it hadn't rung a bell. I felt utterly ashamed as the men recounted the entire incident to Monica and Diana. I was sat with the two loveliest ladies but I'd just been exposed as a thug and now I wanted the ground to swallow me whole.

'I'm sorry I didn't tell you before,' I stammered after the men had gone. 'I used to get into all sorts of trouble, I even spent time inside,' I confessed.

The game was up. I couldn't hide who I really was, so I did the decent thing and came clean.

'I guess you won't want me to help out anymore now, will you?' I asked, my head bowed with shame.

But the silence was pierced with laughter and it was coming from Monica.

'John,' she chuckled. 'I've got a confession too. I was a police officer all my life until recently and I worked the patch where you grew up so I've probably nicked you a few times!'

I shook my head in disbelief. I couldn't see Monica so I guessed I'd never be sure if she had. Still, the thought of it brought a smile to my face because now we were the best of friends. Relief flooded through me; I thought my past had done it again and messed up my fresh start but I was wrong. I was a decent bloke now and together with Dez, I'd prove it. There was only one way and that was up!

Shortly afterwards, I gave my speech and lots of people contacted Guide Dogs offering to be volunteers. I'd made a difference, however small. But I still couldn't get over it, of all the workplaces I could've gone to on my first visit it had to be one I'd got the sack from!

The more visits we did, the more my confidence grew. I particularly loved going into schools and so did Dez. As soon as he saw the children his entire body would shake and his tail would wag. In fact, it wagged so much that sometimes he found it hard to walk in a straight line! He knew what was coming, he loved kids and they loved him back and always smothered him with kisses and cuddles. At one stage I felt him lift up his head to look at me – I knew what he was thinking.

This is the life Dad. Call this work?

Sometimes I felt like his bouncer; the bloke on the other end of his lead. I stood in the background whilst Dez was mobbed by his adoring public.

'How old is he?' a little girl asked.

'Can I stroke him?' said another.

'Oh, I wish I could take him home!' a little voice squealed with excitement.

The children were always the same: as soon as Dez walked into a room, they'd burst with excitement. But, like a true pro, he took it all in his stride. It had been like this since his first brush with showbiz back in the community shop. But now it'd moved up to a whole new level – the Dez fan club.

One day we visited an infants' school. The children were lovely but one in particular touched my heart. After our talk, Dez was mobbed as usual when I heard a little voice behind me. It was coming from a girl aged no more than five.

'Doggy, doggy,' she called.

We'd given lots of guide dog stickers out to the children so we were getting smothered with Transformers ones in return, but I still heard the little girl's voice.

'Do you want to meet Dez,' I called out to her.

The girl didn't answer, but her teacher did.

'I can't believe it,' she gasped. 'This is the first time we've ever heard her speak. It's your dog,' she explained. 'She's besotted by him.'

It later transpired that the little girl had spent her nursery and school life with selective mutism, but Dez had helped her to talk. He really did have an incredible gift.

Soon, Christmas arrived. It was our first one together so I pulled out all the stops and bought him an array of presents including squeaky toys and a bone. After he'd opened them we took a stroll through the village to visit a good friend of mine called Dave Evans. I'd known Dave since I was 16 years old, but now he was in a hospice, terminally ill with a brain tumour. I knew I couldn't let the day pass without going to visit him so off we went. Naturally, the nurses made a fuss of Dez, who was a little hyped up by the time we left, so I took him to some open land so he could let off a bit of steam.

'Happy Christmas mate,' I said as he whooshed off into the distance. By now, I knew Dez and I knew he'd always come back. It had been a very special day indeed.

A few hours later we returned home but then Dez started whimpering and pacing up and down in the front room.

'What's wrong mate?' I asked my voice full of concern.

Dez wasn't himself, he seemed anxious and in distress. It was Christmas Day and I wasn't sure who I could call. In the end I picked up the phone and rang the emergency vet.

'There's something wrong with my dog, please can you help?'

I was so upset that I was almost in tears because I knew Dez was in some sort of pain. I cursed my blindness, if only I could see I'd be able to tell what was wrong with him. The vet sent a dog ambulance over and it whisked Dez away, whilst I sat there alone and bereft by the phone waiting for news. It was the longest night of my life. I didn't even bother going to bed. How could I sleep? My boy was ill. Anxiety clenched inside my stomach like a balled fist and I felt sick with worry. I called the vet yet again for an update.

'I think he's picked something up and eaten it,' he said. 'Whatever it was it hasn't agreed with him so I'll keep him here tonight just for observation.'

Part of me felt relived but the other half was upset. It was our first Christmas together but we'd spent most of it apart. I thought about the open land he'd run on just hours earlier; Dez must have eaten something he'd found but I hadn't been able to see. It wasn't my fault but I blamed myself because I'd failed him.

At 7.30 the following morning the intercom buzzer sounded. It was a nurse from the veterinary practice; she'd brought Dez home. I was so overjoyed but as soon as he walked in through the door I could tell that he wasn't his usual self. He didn't rush in but whimpered as he waddled straight past me and into his bed. He was quite literally as sick as a dog. In the end, I sat up for three solid days and nights nursing him until the sickness subsided. Eventually though I noticed something else. Every feed time he'd jump off the sofa with vigour. He'd had me for a mug, he was better but milking it, playing the drama queen just to win more treats.

'I think you're okay,' I grinned sussing him out.

I felt Dez hang his head: he knew he'd been rumbled. He'd

played me like a fiddle! But all that lack of sleep and sitting with a five-stone hypochondriac dog on my lap had left me with a bloody bad back!

As soon as he was back on form we went out again and Dez's zest for life returned with abundance.

Monica and Diana arranged more visits and we were getting requests from all over; everyone wanted to meet Dez the wonder guide dog!

One day we were asked to go into a pupil referral unit and give a talk to the kids. I knew I was well-suited to it because I knew what it felt like to be them. The first thing I noticed as soon as we walked in was the carpet underneath my feet, but the institutionalised smell was still there. It rose up my nostrils and transported me right back to my troubled youth. It's funny how certain smells remind you of different moments in your life and there was no mistaking this one, a mixture of bleach, arrogance and fear, the smell of hopelessness and of no going back. But now I was here and I was determined to make a difference. We sat down at the front and I began to talk. I spoke candidly to the youngsters and told them all about my troubled past.

'Change your lives now. Do something about it before it's too late.' I begged.

I was determined not to preach but to prove to them it wasn't too late, they could change their own destiny.

'Don't go the same way I did because it will haunt you for the rest of your life. The longer your criminal record, the fewer opportunities you'll have. Take it from someone who knows. Don't do what I did, make that change now.'

By the time I'd finished you could almost hear a pin drop.

Afterwards a few young lads wandered over to speak to me.

'I've got a dog at home and I miss him like mad,' one confessed as he stroked Dez.

'Me too, although mine's not a dog, she's a cat and I miss her. I've had her ever since she was a little kitten,' another said sounding like the child he was.

Dez stood proudly between us and held his head high. I felt proud he was there to help guide me, not just in the physical sense but the emotional sense too. Dez was my anchor, a steady force in my life and, with him by my side, I could now admit to myself and others just how bad my life had been before.

'It's all down to this little fella that I'm still here now,' I said with brutal honesty. 'Without him, who knows where I'd be.'

Within minutes we were surrounded. A dozen hands stretched in to stroke the star of the show – my Dez – and he didn't falter for a second.

'I miss my dog,' another lad said, his voice choked with emotion.

'Me too,' another whispered.

Something had shifted. In that moment there was no pecking order or tough kids, just lads who'd lost their way. Their tough exteriors melted away as, one by one, they revealed themselves and who they really were. People aren't born evil and today had proved that. Dez had reached out to them and somehow touched something inside their hearts and souls. I don't know if we changed the path of anyone's life that day but I hope we made them think about their future.

A month or so later I was at it again, only this time at Leyhill prison in South Gloucestershire. Again, the smell of bleach hit me as soon as we walked inside. It smelt of too many men crammed in together, too much testosterone and bravado, a heady mix of pure intimidation. As soon as the warden slammed the prison gate behind me and turned the key, my stomach churned.

'I never thought I'd find myself back in one of these places quite so soon,' I whispered in Monica's ear. She grabbed my arm and gave it a reassuring squeeze.

We were taken to a room where Diana and Monica talked about the technical side of Guide Dogs and then it was my turn. I knew, like before, that if I wanted people to listen I had to be completely honest. Wrapping an arm around Dez for courage, I cleared my voice and started to speak.

'I know what it's like to do a bit of bird,' I began.

There was a bit of shuffling as the prisoners suddenly sat up in their seats. I knew the score, the inmates used these talks to pass around a bit of contraband but now they'd stopped and I knew I had their full attention. I was later told there were 30 men sat in that room, but each and every one of them listened to my story in all its gory detail.

'I've been in various prisons. My life was a complete mess,' I explained as I began to tell them.

I'm not sure if I made a single jot of difference – these were hardened criminals – but I wanted them to know that there was always hope and Dez had given me my hope back. When I'd finished a few men came over to share their own stories with me. They talked about how much they missed their own families and pets.

All creatures, dogs in particular, seem to strike a chord within people, regardless of age or background. Dogs offer an unconditional kind of love – one that can't be matched. Like children, they become dependent on you but at the same time, they retain their own individual and unique characters. They're a truly unique animal which have the ability to wipe away barriers and bond people together just in conversation. If you've ever owned or loved a dog, you'll know exactly what I mean.

Eventually it was time to leave. As I said goodbye to the men, I prayed that I'd given them hope just as Dez had given me.

Once outside I sighed as the prison gate banged shut behind me. I heard metal scrape against metal as the key turned, only this time, I was on the right side of the fence and it felt great.

As we walked away I inhaled a deep breath of clean air. It'd been a good day and I felt glad to be alive and free.

CHAPTER EIGHTEEN

Sunshine and Rain

NOT LONG AFTER my prison visit, I heard some great news: Suggs was playing a one-man show in Swindon. I knew I had to be there. I bought a ticket and, along with Dez and a friend, took my seat at the back of the theatre. It was a fantastic night although not quite as riotous as the one I remembered from my youth. At the end of the show my friend leaned in to whisper something to me.

'It's Suggs,' he said. 'He's come out to meet people at the front of the stage.'

Soon I was in the same queue, waiting for my moment to speak to one of my all-time heroes only I hoped that this time I'd manage to keep my nerves in check.

Don't call him Mr Suggs this time, you plonker!

Suddenly I was at the front and there he was.

'We've met before,' I told him, shaking his hand warmly.

'Really, where?' Suggs asked.

I explained about the hours I'd spent standing in the freezing cold waiting backstage. I recalled how I'd met him and Lee Thompson but how I'd missed the rest of the band by minutes.

'After the show I jumped on your bus, like a nutter,' I grinned, sounding like a 44-year-old teenager.

Suggs laughed too.

'And who's this?' he asked, stooping down to give Dez a pat on the head.

'This is Dez.' I announced proudly as I told him all about my wonderful boy. I felt honoured that such a great man had been interested in me and Dez. He was and is a true gentleman.

'Well, you look after yourself John,' he said tapping the top of my arm before he left. Suggs didn't realise it but he'd just made my day.

With my confidence at an all time high I decided to do some serious fundraising for Guide Dogs.

'I'm going to do a sponsored swim,' I announced to Diana and Monica. 'Ten miles in ten days, but I need to get fit first.'

My enthusiasm may have been commendable but actually getting my knackered old body into a freezing cold pool to do the swim was quite another thing. I needed to get fit and fast! One day, I strolled into Thornbury Leisure Centre and asked the lady behind reception if she'd watch Dez whilst I practised in the pool. I felt Dez look up at me as if I'd lost the plot. He knew I was no athlete. But there was an added bonus to my training regime and a few days later his paws were well and truly under the table as the staff fussed around him. If only the swimming had been as easy.

On my first day I planned to swim ten lengths but managed only two. When I came out of the male changing room I felt a little deflated but Dez cheered me up. As soon as he heard my footsteps I heard him get to his feet, take a running jump and hurtle over the top of the counter and into the foyer.

'Hey boy, have you missed me?' I laughed ruffling the fur at the back of his ears.

'He's been as good as gold!' the manageress said coming over to greet me. 'But as soon as he heard you he was up and over the counter like greased lightning!'

'So, you won't mind watching him again for me while I practice?'

'No, not at all. He's a real pleasure, aren't you Dez?'

The next time we went Dez was so excited to see his new pals that he almost dragged me inside.

'Dez!' they shouted in unison as soon we walked in through the door. His tail swished in the air like a mini helicopter.

With a little practice, I managed to increase my two lengths to ten. The more I swam the stronger I was until I not only became more streamlined in the water but I felt it too. But just as I'd started to improve so I began to feel very unwell. My body was crippled with a pain in my back that radiated to one side. I was such agony that I couldn't swim, so I called Yvonne. She was Dez's boarder and had looked after him as a puppy. I needed to know he was okay before I got myself to hospital. Once he was settled, I was taken to Southmead Hospital where doctors prescribed pain relief and ordered an X-ray. But I missed my pal and without him, I felt so alone. The X-ray revealed I had a kidney stone but I didn't care, I just wanted to be with Dez, so I spoke to a nurse who rang Yvonne for me.

'Do you want me to bring him in to visit you? I don't mind,' Yvonne suggested.

Mind? I could've kissed her!

Once I knew Dez was on his way I started to relax and even chat up the nurses.

'Wait until you see my Dez,' I boasted, 'As soon as he sees me he'll be all over me like a rash, just you watch. You've never seen anything like it. We're a team; I bet he's missed me as much as I have him.'

Soon I heard the familiar pitter-patter of paws on the ward. My face lit up as soon as I heard him bound over towards me.

'Here he is,' I announced. I climbed off my bed and knelt down on the floor in readiness. With my arms outstretched I waited for him to fly into my embrace. 'Here's my boy!'

His paws tapped even louder as he approached. I waited for the full force of his body and rush of love. I held out my hands ready to give him the biggest cuddle of his life... but he scurried straight past. To add insult to injury, I even felt the slight whip of his tail as he pushed past me in his hurry to get to the nurses.

'Hello Dez!' they cooed behind me. 'We've been hearing all about you!'

Dez had used his lethal brown eyes, I guessed because the nurses had melted into one gigantic puddle behind me. Like the heartthrob he is, he'd hooked the lot of them. It took a few minutes but finally, when he'd exhausted all the free strokes and love, he sauntered casually over towards me.

Oh, hi Dad. Didn't notice you there, he sniffed coolly.

'You bloody ladies' man!' I huffed as I patted him on the back.

The nurses laughed and so did the rest of the ward. He'd just made me look like a right old plonker.

But with Dez by my side I was soon fit and healthy and

back on my feet. I returned to the pool but then I suffered another setback; an ingrown toenail.

'I'm turning into an old man Dez,' I moaned as I hobbled to the doctor to get it sorted.

I could just imagine Dez rolling his eyes and shaking his head in despair.

After a small op, I was told to keep my foot dry for six weeks. I felt frustrated but as it turned out I needed to be elsewhere. Dave's condition had worsened since Christmas. Although Dez and I had continued to visit regularly, I knew time was running out.

Dave had been such a good friend to me over the years that it broke my heart to think I was finally losing him.

We'd first met when we were teenagers. I'd started a stupid argument with him but Dave refused to hold a grudge and instead, went out of his way to save me from myself. One day there was some trouble. A few kids had come over from a different estate to pick fights. I wanted revenge and, fired up by my other so-called mates I travelled to the village pub where I knew the gang hung out. I was out of control, the local nutter, and this time I'd gone armed because I knew I'd be outnumbered. There were five or six of them but I had no one who was willing to back me up so I tucked a lump hammer into the back pocket of my jeans. High on booze, I was just about to push my way into the rival pub when I felt something slide out of my back pocket. My hand felt behind but it had gone. I turned in bewilderment to see Dave running away – he had the hammer in his hands.

'Give me that back,' I shouted after him. I was livid he'd scuppered my plans.

'No John, I won't let you do it. You'll kill yourself or someone else.' Dave reasoned.

I was fuming but Dave refused to listen.

'You'll end up in prison John, it's not worth it,' he called back to me as he ran away.

I gave chase but Dave was sober and faster than me. To begin with I was furious; it was only later when I sobered up that I thanked him.

'I don't deserve a mate like you,' I said shaking my head in shame.

'Don't be daft,' he said. 'Someone's got to keep an eye on you because none of your so-called mates will.'

As I grew older I often thought back to that moment, the day Dave saved my life, so I was delighted when I heard he'd settled down with a lovely girl called Louise. They tried for a baby but as soon as he discovered he was going to be a father fate chose to snatch his joy away with the other hand.

'I've got a brain tumour John,' Dave told me.

The news crushed me but Dave being Dave was more concerned about my well-being than his own. Eventually he was transferred to a hospice. Thankfully, it wasn't far from where I lived so, as soon as I was able, I took Dez along to meet him. Dave had always been there for me and now it was my turn to repay the favour.

As Dave's son Oscar grew into a beautiful little boy, so my lovely mate succumbed to the ravages of cancer. Dave loved Dez almost as much as I did and the three of us would spend many hours together talking about the past and the future.

One day Dave turned to me. Dez was nestled in between us as if he was listening to every single word.

'Promise me something, John,' Dave began.

'Anything,' I replied taking his hand.

'Promise me that no matter how bad things get you'll never turn back to drink again. Do it for me John, do it for Dez, but most importantly do it for yourself.'

Tears pricked at the back of my eyes as I nodded and made a solemn vow to my friend. Dez and I remained by his side right up to the very end, but on 18 April 2012, my best friend Dave Evans lost his fight for life. His son was just three years old.

I still miss Dave every day. He was a top bloke, a quietly spoken man and the complete opposite of me. He gave everyone his time and he cared for others like no one else I know. Dave didn't care for petty arguments or fallouts, all he cared about was his family and his mates and I'm proud that he chose me as his friend. Even today, when faced with a problem I often find myself thinking, *What would Dave say?*

If I can be half the man Dave was then I'll die happy. His partner Louise later told me how proud he'd had been because I'd managed to turn my life around and that he wanted me to keep my promise to him. I have, and I will continue to do so because I gave him my word.

Spurred on by my friend's death, I vowed to do some good and complete my marathon swim. As soon as I could I was back in the pool, swimming every day. I was doing this for Dez, for the charity but most of all I was doing it for Dave. He'd saved my life and now it was time to put my battered old body to good use. Life was too short for moping around, Dave had taught me that, but now I could do something that would really make a difference.

The first day of the swim was tough and it took me well over two hours but as my body readjusted, each mile got easier until finally I completed my last mile in less than 45 minutes. I'd raised over £1,000 for Guide Dogs even though my target had been £500. I'd completely smashed it because the community shop had been taking sponsors and had managed to collect £360 from generous Almondsbury residents alone. I was thrilled. Every single penny raised from the swim went to Guide Dogs.

For the first time in ages I felt proud of myself and all I'd achieved. What I didn't realise then was that all my efforts were about to be eclipsed by something much bigger than I could have ever imagined.

CHAPTER NINETEEN

Man's Best Friend

ONE DAY MONICA called round to see me.

'John,' she said, her voice rising with excitement. 'You and Dez have been nominated for a Life Changing Award at the annual Guide Dogs ceremony in London.'

'No way,' I gasped. I shook my head in disbelief; Dez had certainly changed my life but I thought I was the only one who'd noticed.

'Are you sure?'

'Well, I should be,' she quipped, 'because I'm the one who nominated you.'

I chuckled.

'But John,' she continued. 'I'm pleased to say you've won!'

I gasped again.

'This is why I've come to see you. There's going to be an awards ceremony in London and I need you both to come with me.'

I was astonished. Monica had played her cards close to her chest because it had all been booked, the train and the hotel. Soon the morning arrived for us to travel down to London. My mind flashed back to my last train journey home from the capital when I'd just been told the devastating news I was blind. I shuddered as I recalled how I'd almost drunk myself to death on the journey. Now, 17 months later here I was, on my way to London with Dez so we could collect our award.

Thankfully, I already owned a good suit that was lurking at the bottom of my wardrobe. It needed a dry clean but soon it was as good as new. I packed it up and together with Monica and Dez we stepped on the train and headed for the city.

Later that evening in my hotel room as I pulled on my best suit I started to snigger because the irony wasn't lost on me. I felt Dez look up at me, probably wondering why I was laughing.

'This feels weird,' I confessed, 'because this is the only time I've worn this suit and not been standing in a court dock.'

Of course Dez didn't understand or care as long as I gave him a good brush so he too could look his best.

'Don't worry mate,' I joked. 'I've brought your chamois leather with me!'

An hour later we were sat at a table inside a big room. Adrian Chiles was compere for the evening and as I listened to one remarkable story after another, I wondered what I was doing there. Guide Dogs had helped enrich so many people's lives but they were all so much more deserving than an oik like me. I was happy for Dez because unlike his owner, he deserved all the credit. Besides, he wasn't one to miss out on attention or the chance to have his photo taken. Soon it was our turn to take to the stage and when Dez and I were presented with the Life Changing Award, a lump formed at the back of my throat because I realised just how far we'd come.

'Well done, boy.' I said giving the fur on top of his head a quick ruffle. I felt so proud of him I thought I'd burst.

I was just about to go back to my seat when someone told me to stay on stage. All the finalists in the four different categories had been nominated for the prestigious Guide Dog of the Year award. It didn't matter to me because Dez was already a champion in my eyes but I did as I was told and waited along with the other finalists. I convinced myself that we'd come fourth out of four, not because of Dez, but because of me. We stood there as each finalist's story was told to the audience using a short film. The more I listened, the more emotional I became – this truly was the most fantastic charity.

I heard our names called out as a short film rolled on a screen at the back of the stage. It'd been filmed back in Bristol when someone from Guide Dogs had come along to capture us together on a walk. The film had only just got started when I heard a peal of laughter. All of a sudden the whole audience was in an uproar. I knew exactly which bit of the film they were watching; the part where Dez bounced off the lead into a field of long grass like a kangaroo! I knew because as the cameraman filmed it, he couldn't stop laughing. Although I couldn't see it, I pictured it frame by frame in my head. Dez's infectious character had won them over just like everyone else we'd ever met.

With all the films shown, it was now down to Adrian Chiles to announce the winner. To be honest I just wanted it to be over so Dez and I could sit back down. It was tiring standing there and we were both sweating underneath the bright spotlights. I knew we had absolutely no chance of winning.

There was a tense rustle and rip of paper sounded through the microphone as Adrian ripped opened the envelope in his hands.

'And the winner of Guide Dog of the Year 2012 is...'

He paused and it seemed to take forever. My feet were killing me and the collar of my shirt felt too tight against my neck.

'The winner is... Dez!'

What?

I clasped a hand over my mouth in astonishment.

Did I just hear him right? Did he just call out Dez's name?

My heart stopped as someone stepped forward and thrust a microphone into my hand.

'Congratulations,' she whispered.

The microphone felt sweaty in my palm and, for once in my life, I was speechless. I was so dumbstruck that I hadn't prepared a single thing to say.

'Err,' I stammered. Cheers and wild applause echoed around the room. It was so loud that it took a while to calm down. I stood there frozen in the middle of the stage like a startled rabbit caught in headlights. Even as the applause subsided I was still lost for words when I felt something nudge against my leg – it was Dez. He lifted his head up as if acknowledging the applause; this was his moment, not mine, and I couldn't let him down.

'Err...' I began awkwardly again, momentarily thrown by the volume of my voice through the mic.

'Thank you so much, Dez and I are absolutely delighted

with this award. What can I say? It's quite a shock,' I told them truthfully.

The audience laughed, it was clear it was a complete shock. I smiled before continuing: 'There's one person and one person alone who we'd like to dedicate this award to and that is Emma Yard, our brilliant mobility instructor. Without her, we wouldn't be here today.'

Once again I was glad of my dark glasses because underneath my eyes were flooded with tears. I could hardly believe it – less than 18 months ago I'd convinced myself that my life was over and that all hope was lost but it wasn't. For now I had Dez and wonderful people, like Emma, Monica, Diana and so many more behind me every step of the way. To be honest, I don't know how I got off stage because I was so elated and high on emotion. It had been quite a night and, as it later transpired, one that Monica had known all about for a while. But she'd kept it quiet – once a copper...

Afterwards, Dez and I were inundated with requests from the press. There were photographers all wanting to take a picture of Dez. Adrian Chiles knelt down and handed my pal a great big biscuit bone. Dez fell in love with Adrian instantly because he'd fed him. He slurped as he gobbled up the treat greedily.

'Can you get Dez to look up at the camera John?' a photographer called.

I tried but Dez wasn't having any of it. He loved the stardom and all attention which went with it but right now his bone was so much more appealing. In true showbiz style, the photographers had to hang around and wait until Dez the diva had finished his bone. But, once the flashbulbs went off there was no stopping him and he posed like a professional.

'I think he's done this before,' someone quipped.

'He has!' I shouted back, grinning like an idiot.

After our photo shoot I was interviewed by journalists from the BBC, various dog magazines, the RNIB, and of course Guide Dogs. At first I felt a little nervous and stumbled over my words but I recounted my story to each and every one of them.

'He's my life,' I told them all. 'I wouldn't be here without Dez.'

I felt him huff at my side and heard his voice in my head. *Blah, blah, blah. Yes, I'm wonderful…Oh no, he's off again!*

I started to chuckle because I knew I was starting to sound like a broken record. Even though I was busy singing his praises, I could hear him sniffing around on the floor looking for biscuits. He was such a superstar that I don't know how I got his head or his ego out of the room that night!

The following day, on the train back home to Bristol, I was still on such a high that I couldn't wipe the grin off my face. My Dez, Guide Dog of the Year. I couldn't wait to tell them all back home. Of course everyone was delighted and, like a proud dad, I bored them all to death bragging about how perfect he was. But, true to form, it didn't take long for his halo to slip.

A week or so later we were in the bank when I started to tell the ladies all about Dez's win.

'He's such a star and so well behaved,' I told them.

The ladies in the bank loved Dez and fussed over him. A few minutes later, we turned to leave.

'Bye then,' I called as Dez led the way. But as we neared the automatic door he suddenly stopped. I presumed the queue for the bus stop was right up to the building and that's when I heard it, a loud crunching noise. There was laughter all around, the ladies in the bank and all the people at the bus stop; everyone was in hysterics. I felt down with my hand and realised Dez was eating something; it felt crumbly and sticky against my fingers, it was a muesli bar.

'I'm ever so sorry,' a lady said rushing over to me. 'My child fed him that when my back was turned.'

I tried not to laugh – at least he hadn't nicked it this time! Still, I was horrified that my 'wonderful Dez' had disgraced himself yet again. Typical Labrador – he'd be bloody useless on a diet!

Following his award, Dez was in demand and busier than ever with everyone wanting to meet my famous dog. So, a short while later, when a friend invited us up to Scotland for the weekend, I jumped at the chance. I reckoned the break would do us both good. It was to be my longest journey to date and I felt a little apprehensive but deep down I knew I was ready. I telephoned ahead, booking assistance at every station. The journey involved two train changes, one at Birmingham and one in Carlisle. The first part of the journey went smoothly but as we pulled into Birmingham station, I realised Dez hadn't had a wee for a few hours. I asked a member of staff if he'd take us out to the front of the station so Dez could go to the toilet. Anyone who's ever walked through Birmingham New Street station will tell you, it's a maze, especially to a blind man and his dog, but finally we reached the pavement outside.

'Come on Dez. Busy busy,' I said using my guide dog command for him to pee on cue but Dez was having none of it.

'Has he done yet?' I asked the guy standing beside me.

He dipped forward to get a better look.

'Nope, not yet.'

'Come on Dez, busy busy,' I said once more. I listened and waited but nothing, not even a drop.

The next train journey to Carlisle was five hours long so I needed Dez to go and to go now.

'Come on mate,' I coaxed, 'this could be your last chance to go.'

The harness shifted a little as Dez looked up at me but he just wasn't interested so we walked back inside to catch our next train. The next journey was long but Dez was as good as gold. He sat at my feet the whole time but popped his head up occasionally whenever anyone went by; he was a genius when it came to getting a free stroke or ear rub. I listened out but he didn't squirm or potter around, all the usual signs that he needed the toilet. Instead, he rested his head on his paws and basked in the adoration.

Surely, he must need to go by now? I thought.

I wondered where he was storing it all; maybe Dez was a camel and no one had told me.

Hours later we pulled into Carlisle station but Dez was as chilled out as ever. Sure enough, someone was there to meet me so I immediately asked how to get out to the front.

'I need to go outside the station because my dog needs...'

Suddenly, and from nowhere, my words were interrupted by the deafening sound of gushing water. It was so loud, it drowned me out and it went on so long that it sounded as if someone was filling up a bath! With my mouth agog I waited until Dez had finished weeing. And then I waited some more. Around thirty seconds later, he finally stopped.

'I'm so sorry,' I told the guard. 'He's been on the train for ages but he wouldn't go at Birmingham.'

But the man interrupted me.

'It's okay mate,' he chuckled. 'Everyone does that here.'

'What?' I said as quick as a flash. 'Dogs or humans?'

We were both in hysterics as I carefully tiptoed over the huge puddle that Dez had created. It was so large that he'd almost flooded the platform!

Hours later, I arrived safe and sound in Scotland. I couldn't believe just how friendly and helpful everyone had been, even though my perfect Guide Dog of the Year had disgraced himself. After that we started catching the train all over the country. Dez and I were on a roll and now there was no stopping us!

However, not everyone was as helpful or indeed very kind. One morning I caught the bus back to Frampton Cotterell to visit my sister Clair. It was a two bus journey but I liked the independence of being able to travel on my own with Dez. So, when Clair offered me a lift back home I politely refused. Dez and I left her house and headed back up towards the bus stop. We were only a few streets away when I heard a voice call from behind.

'You got any spare change mate?'

But I didn't.

'Sorry mate, I haven't,' I told him and continued along the pavement.

However, instead of simply moving on the man started to follow us.

'Go on, I bet you have,' he said sneaking up behind, hissing in my ear.

I flinched and Dez sensed it. I'd never felt vulnerable

before but I did now. But I didn't want this idiot to know so I ignored him but walked a little faster.

Who in their right mind would ask a blind man for money? I thought to myself.

There was clearly something very wrong here. I didn't know for sure but I guessed he was a junkie. At that moment he started to giggle, like a goblin. It confirmed it; he was definitely off his head on something.

'Behind you,' he cooed.

He called from far away and then ran up right behind me and shouted loudly in my ear to make me jump. I started to get a bit freaked out, Dez sensed my fear but continued on the harness and tried his best to get us out of there. Then, without warning, the man started running up behind us and stamping his feet as hard as he could on the ground. Dez whimpered because the man was spooking him out now, it made me furious.

'Leave us alone.' I shouted.

Suddenly, I felt a hand on my shoulder as he shoved me forwards. I stumbled but didn't fall. Dez whimpered loudly in front of me; I could tell he was frightened and not sure what to do. He'd devoted his entire life to protecting me but no amount of training could prepare him for something like this.

'Listen,' I said turning to face the man. 'If you don't clear off I'm calling the police.'

'Oooh!' his voice mocked.

My stomach knotted inside. I knew there was a church up ahead and it was surrounded by tall hedges, I was worried he'd use them to jump out in front of us. Despite my constant threats the man refused to leave us alone. And that's when it happened. Dez was so stressed that he stepped out right into the middle of the road. I was flabbergasted. This man had obviously absolutely terrified him because, apart from saving my life, he'd never done it before. The Green Cross Code dog had just broken his golden rule. I knew we couldn't continue. Dez was in such a state that I stopped walking and tried to flag a car down.

I waited for the man to jump out, shout or do something but instead there was an eerie silence. After what seemed like an age, a car finally slowed and stopped. I thanked the driver and told him all about the idiot.

'Well, there's no one here now but hop in and I'll take you to the bus stop.'

'Thanks,' I said gratefully as we climbed in.

A few minutes later, we pulled up at the bus stop and I was just about to climb out of the car when the junkie reappeared.

'Got any money mate?' he asked the driver.

'Is this him?' the Good Samaritan asked. I nodded my head.

'That's it,' I said. 'I'm calling the police right now.'

I'd had my run-ins with the police in the past but now, when I really needed them they arrived on the scene like a shot. Officers scoured the area but couldn't find the man; however they kept in touch to make sure I was okay. Once again it restored my faith in the police force. It truly felt good to be on the right side of the law.

If I thought that was going to be a one-off incident, I was wrong. A month later, I was in the city centre. I was dying of thirst and needed to buy a fizzy drink so I walked into the nearest newsagent shop. I was just about to enter the store when I heard someone shouting and then I realised it was the shopkeeper – he was shouting at me. I heard someone in front of me and I felt a hand against my chest as he started to push and shove me out of his shop. Dez was so alarmed he didn't know what to do.

'No, no, no!' the shopkeeper screamed. He was so loud that everyone in the shop had turned to look. 'Get out of my shop. I'm not having that fucking animal in here!'

For a split second I was stunned into silence but then my blood started to boil; that was my Dez he was talking about.

'He's a guide dog,' I said. 'He's allowed. I'm blind. It's against the law not to let us in.'

Other people in the shop backed me up but the shopkeeper wouldn't listen.

'I don't care, take that filthy animal out of here.'

'Right,' I said, a rage rising up like a volcano inside me. The man was lucky; in the old days I would have lashed out at him but not today because now I was a changed man. Instead I got out my mobile phone and called the police. Sure enough, they arrived minutes later. I explained the situation, and thankfully I was backed up by people inside the shop. The police listened to both sides and informed the shopkeeper that he was breaking the law. Also, because he'd forcibly pushed me out onto the street he'd also assaulted me into the bargain.

'Do you want to press charges?' an officer asked me.

'No,' I replied. 'I just want him to realise what he's done – he's breaking the law.'

In the end the shopkeeper apologised and even invited me inside but I refused to give him my custom. After that, you wouldn't have got me in his shop for all the tea in China.

'No thanks,' I sniffed. 'I think we'll go somewhere else.'

As I turned to walk away one of the police officers stopped me and pulled me to one side.

'I wouldn't mind,' he said, his voice quiet and low, 'but there's even a sign in his shop window which says 'no dogs, only guide dogs allowed'.'

'Priceless,' I scoffed. And it was. You couldn't make it up.

But Dez didn't care, as long as I was alright. He just took it in his stride and rose above it. He knew as well as I did there are some people in life who aren't worth bothering with.

In fact the more time I spent with him, the more I realised that Dez was so much more than a guide dog and my eyes on the world. Not only was he my best friend but he was my protector too, always by my side when things got tough. There was no way I'd let a few idiots upset or intimidate us. I knew Dez had been trained not to react but I was certain if something happened, he'd step in.

'Do you think Dez would ever protect you if you were in danger?' a friend asked me afterwards.

'He would,' I insisted. 'But I wouldn't want him to because if danger was coming I'd risk my own life to save his.'

I felt Dez's head lift underneath my arm as he looked up at me. I couldn't see his lovely brown eyes but I didn't have to because I knew they were full of love, and the feeling was mutual.

'Come here boy,' I said pulling him in close for a cuddle. I smiled as he moulded his warm body next to mine on the sofa. His head nuzzled in right underneath my chin and I felt his breath on my neck as he let out a contented sigh.

I smiled as I thought how many times we'd broken that rule, no pets on the furniture, but I didn't care. Dez wasn't my pet or even my dog, he was my best pal and we had a unique bond and it was one which would never be broken.

CHAPTER TWENTY

A Dog Called Dez

A FEW MONTHS LATER, we were invited to give a speech at a charity quiz night for Guide Dogs. Diana asked me to do it and I didn't hesitate; the more money and awareness we could raise, the better.

As usual, I groomed Dez's coat to make sure he looked smart for his next stint on stage. By now he was used to the limelight and there were times when I just felt like a prop in the background. People had come to see Dezzy Boy, not me, and rightly so. When our moment came we were taken up onto the stage. Once there, I started to tell the audience just how wonderful Dez was and what he'd done for me. If I'm honest, I bragged a little, like any proud parent would. I not only gushed about how amazing Dez was but also how well-behaved he was too.

'He's so well-disciplined, it's unbelievable,' I told the packed crowd, conveniently forgetting his recent brush with the muesli bar outside the bank.

I couldn't see them but I'd been told the hall was filled with around 200 people. It had been a lovely evening and we'd thoroughly enjoyed ourselves. I felt stuffed too because they'd even laid on a delicious buffet.

After I'd finished my speech, Dez walked forward and we left the stage to a round of applause. It was still ringing in my ears when the lady who had helped us up there grabbed my arm to help lead me back to my seat.

'No,' I tried to tell her, 'I'm fine, honestly, I can manage.'

The thing with some guide dogs, and I'm particularly talking about Dez here, is as soon as another person comes to my aid by linking my arm he immediately clocks off work. Although this lady meant well, what she didn't realise was that, as soon as she grabbed my arm, she'd given Dez the green light to go. Within a split second he went from being 'Guide Dog of the Year' to a regular naughty boy. As we made our way back to my table my arm shot out to the side. I heard a few people laugh and within seconds the whole place was in an uproar.

'Your dog has just jumped onto the buffet table and snatched a piece of chocolate cake,' the lady whispered in my ear.

'Dez!' I shouted.

I tried my best to retrieve the cake but he was quicker than me and by the time I got to him all that was left was crumbs around his mouth.

'Naughty boy,' I scolded in my softest voice. I wanted the ground to swallow me up. I'd just spent a good five minutes telling everyone how wonderful he was only for him to go and blow it! By the time we reached the table everyone was in hysterics, especially Diana and Allie, another fundraiser from Guide Dogs. You could have fried an egg on the red hot heat coming off my face; talk about showing me up!

If I thought Dez winning Guide Dog of the Year was going to be the only highlight of my life, I was wrong. I'd booked my tickets for the House of Fun weekender, which is a must for all die-hard Madness fans. During one weekend we took over Butlins in Minehead, as around 6,000 fans filled every single room on the camp. I was there with Dez but, unbeknownst to me, a friend had organised something and gone the extra mile to make my visit just that little bit more special.

I was sat with Dez in Butlins cinema listening to a Madness film when I heard someone approach.

'Hello, you must be John,' a voice said, breaking my concentration. 'I'm Chris Foreman.'

At first I thought it was a wind-up. Chrissy Boy or Chris Foreman was the guitarist in Madness and it couldn't be him. But my friend who was sitting beside me confirmed it was indeed the man himself. I was completely thrown until my mate explained how he'd emailed Chris via the Madness website to arrange the meeting. I was stunned and thrilled all at the same time. I told Chris how much I admired him and the other lads in the band.

'Minehead is where it all started for me,' I explained, recounting my time in the special school unit with my skinhead mates. 'It's where I first got into Madness so coming here today is a bit like coming home for me.'

Chris asked me lots of questions and I soon found myself telling him about my life and how I'd lost my sight.

'But this young fella's saved my life,' I said patting Dez on the back. 'I wouldn't be here without him now.'

Once I started I couldn't stop. I proudly explained how Dez had won Guide Dog of the Year, and before long I was gushing on about Madness again.

'You've always been there for me with your songs; they've helped me through the darkest days of my life,' I insisted. 'The thought that I'd come back to hear another Madness gig again has kept me going...'

'Aww, don't,' Chris laughed making out he'd just wiped away a tear from his eye. 'You'll have me crying in a minute.'

With that we all started to laugh, although it was clear he'd been touched by my story.

'Anyway, it's been good to meet you John,' he said finally, shaking my hand.

'You too, and thanks,' I told him.

I thought all my birthdays had come at once and, try as I might, I just couldn't wipe the daft grin off my face. Dez was staring at me as if I'd completely lost the plot and, in many ways I had. I was delirious with happiness. I was still on cloud nine when a few moments later someone else tapped me on the shoulder; it was someone from the band's management team.

'Chris wondered if you wanted to come backstage and meet the rest of the band?'

'What?' I gasped. I couldn't believe this was really happening.

But it was. I was still trembling with excitement as we were led into the VIP area at the back of the stage. Moments later, Dez and I were taken into the Madness dressing room. It was only half an hour before the show and the band was busy psyching themselves up for their performance. Still, each and every one of them came over and shook my hand. In fact, they went out of their way to give me and Dez a warm welcome. Out of the blue I heard a familiar voice.

'Hello, its Suggs here,' he said as he shook my hand warmly.

'Yes,' I gushed, my voice rising with excitement as I recalled, 'we met last year.'

'Yes, I remember you!'

I was thrilled until I realised that Suggs was patting Dez on top of the head. He remembered him more than me! But then, Dez was the star of the show and without him I was just another face in the crowd, another nutty boy! It didn't matter because I was here right now, with Dez and with Madness.

Then I heard another voice, it belonged to Lee Thompson, my all-time hero. We started to chat and I shared my story. Lee sympathised because he'd had a tough upbringing too, it was this which had inspired some of his greatest songs. Blind but totally starry-eyed, I spent a good 25 minutes backstage with the band chatting until the time came for them to go on stage.

'Thanks,' I shouted as I turned to leave. I was grinning like a kid in a sweet shop but I couldn't help it. 'You've made my year lads, you really have.'

'Bye John, enjoy the show.' they called after me.

'I will!' I grinned.

One of the management team led Dez and me back out to the front.

'We'll be fine from here,' I insisted as I thanked him for his help.

Soon I was back out in the real world with all the other Madness fans. Walking up the ramp, Dez and I found our way to my seat situated on the raised disabled platform. I knew we'd be safe up here – we wouldn't get bumped into – but we were still at the centre of it all. I took a deep breath and soaked up the atmosphere. It didn't matter that I wasn't at the front of the stage now. Even if I had been fully-sighted I doubt it would have topped this moment because I'd just had my very own private audience with Madness.

Suddenly a roar almost lifted off the roof. It was so loud that it sounded as though an earthquake had erupted. Madness was on.

Chas's voice boomed over the mic, '*Hey you, don't watch that, watch this! This is the heavy heavy monster sound… One Step Beyond.*'

The roar was so loud that my chair shook along with the ground beneath my feet as vibrations rattled through the floor. An electric tingle ran down my spine and the hair on the back of my neck stood up as Lee's saxophone kicked in and everyone started to stomp. I was right there in the moment and boy, it felt good.

Resting my left hand down, I patted Dez lovingly on his neck. His fur was soft and silky beneath my touch as I pulled him close and kissed him on his big, gorgeous, square head. He rested it blissfully against my lap. I sighed with pure and utter joy because I knew whatever happened after this moment, with Dez by my side and the best group in the world on stage, life simply couldn't get better than this.

Acknowledgements

THERE ARE SO many people I'd like to thank that I don't really know where to begin so I'd like to start with my amazing son James – you are the finest son a father could ever wish to have, thank you for making me so proud, I love you with all my heart.

To my wonderful sister Clair, her husband Paul Chappell, and their brilliant kids Danny, Billy, Kelly, Molly and Jamie. Thank you to Tracey and Phil Winter-Alsop and their beautiful girls Pippa and Sophie (my unofficial nieces) for never giving up on me, and also Trevor and Jackie Watkins.

To all my friends who helped me through my darkest days especially the ones who dragged me back out into the world when all I wanted to do was crawl under a rock and die, namely Liza and Kevin Baker, Bob and Katherine German, and Hannah Rowley and Paul Kilbie. Also to Louise and Oscar – I know Dave will be looking down on us all with pride.

There are so many people I'd like to mention at the Guide Dogs charity but I haven't enough space so, my heartfelt thanks goes to Monica and Roger Cave (cheers for the computer software Roger, which has helped me 'read' this book). Diana and Dave Mager, Allie Selby, Viv Jones, Yvonne Dutton, and Verna and David Clifford – you've all played such an important part in getting me back on my feet again. My heartfelt thanks to Adam, my counsellor from RNIB, and Clara Markwick, who taught me long cane training and gave me my mobility back.

But my eternal gratitude must go to the wonderful Emma Yard, without whom I wouldn't be where I am today. Thanks Emma, from both me and Dez. You truly are one in a million and the work you do everyday transforms other people's lives – we owe you everything.

To my ghostwriter Veronica Clark, who read my mind and penned every word in this book. Veronica helped guide me through what was at times an emotional but fulfilling experience. We agreed from the very beginning that this would be a true and honest account of my past, warts and all, but she's made me realise just how far I've come in my life. Thanks Veronica, you've had me crying and laughing in equal measure and I can't praise you or your writing skills enough.

Veronica would also like me to thank Lauren Abrokwah and Kathryn Herbst at the Guide Dogs Training Centre in Leamington Spa, who not only helped her research the book but also made her a lovely cuppa on a freezing cold day!

To all the residents of Almondsbury, there are too many to mention but here's a few: all the people in the community village shop, especially Angela, Gill, Jenny, Deborah, Alun

ACKNOWLEDGEMENTS

and Geoff. To my amazing friends: Fiona and Ian, Anita and Phil and Brian and Vicky, who have supported me.

Thanks to Liz Mallett and all the team at John Blake Publishing for believing in my story and giving me the chance to share it.

My huge gratitude to Madness – in my opinion the best band in the world! This band doesn't only pen brilliant songs; it's formed the musical backdrop to my life and has always given me hope.

Last but not least, the biggest credit has to go to my amazing guide dog Dez. My four-legged pal not only gave me back my life but also taught me how to live again.

Please Help

I'M DONATING ALL my profits from this book to the Guide Dogs charity because it changes the lives of people every single day. If you would like to volunteer for this wonderful organisation or donate funds to help pay for more dogs like Dez, please contact **www.guidedogs.org.uk**

To sponsor or name a puppy please call: **0870 2406993**
For all other enquiries contact: **01189 835555**

Thank you.
John and Dez
May 2013